FINISHING WELL,
FINISHING STRONG

OTHER BOOKS BY
DR. JAMES GRASSI

Guts, Grace, and Glory
The Ultimate Men's Ministry Encyclopedia
A Study Guide of Israel
Crunch Time
Crunch Time in the Red Zone
Wading Through the Chaos
The Ultimate Hunt
In Pursuit of the Prize
Heaven on Earth
The Ultimate Fishing Challenge
The Spiritual Mentor
Building a Ministry of Spiritual Mentoring
More Than a Fisherman

Men's Ministry Catalyst Website:
www.mensministrycatalyst.org

FINISHING WELL, FINISHING STRONG

BY JIM **GRASSI**

THOMAS NELSON
Since 1798

NASHVILLE   DALLAS   MEXICO CITY   RIO DE JANEIRO

Published in Nashville, Tennessee, by Thomas Nelson. Thomas Nelson is a registered trademark of HarperCollins Christian Publishing, Inc.

Page design and layout: Crosslin Creative

Thomas Nelson titles may be purchased in bulk for educational, business, fund-raising, or sales promotional use. For information, please e-mail SpecialMarkets@ThomasNelson.com.

Printed in the United States of America

14 15 16 17 18 RRD 5 4 3 2 1

DEDICATION

We started our national ministry over three decades ago. One of the first people I consulted was a middle-aged pastor whom I met at a family camp who impressed me with his insights, directness, wisdom, and wit. Dr. Chuck Swindoll soon became a mentor and friend. Distance and time have separated us from regular meetings, but through his occasional notes of encouragement, timely messages, and international radio programs, he has remained a consistent model of someone who knows God and desires to serve Him with all his heart.

He is a faithful model of Christlikeness and has shepherded millions with his authentic and transparent life. He is a man whose life transcends our culture and who has set an example for all of us to follow. His is a life that models the message of this book. Chuck's obedient heart testifies to a life well lived. Certainly he is a man who will "finish well and finish strong."

His contributions and continued work in God's vineyard remind us all that we have a purpose in God's plan for redeeming this broken world. It is to this humble servant of God whose significant eternal contributions are beyond our comprehension that I dedicate this book. Thanks Pastor Chuck and all those who want to finish well and strong for reminding all of us to stay in the battle for men's souls.

Each of us has been blessed with specific gifts, talents, opportunities, experiences, and abilities to be used of God for His glory (Eph. 4:11–16). It is our delight and honor to serve our Lord and multiply what He has given us. It is not a duty or obligation, but a privilege and joy.

"Whatever we do for ourselves dies with us. What we do for others and the world remains and is immortal."

—Albert Pike [1]

CONTENTS

	Introduction	ix
Chapter 1:	What It Means to Finish Well and Strong	**1**
Chapter 2:	Start Well to Finish Well	**9**
Chapter 3:	The Dash on My Tombstone	**17**
Chapter 4:	How Do I Measure Success?	**26**
Chapter 5:	Success, Significance, or Both?	**34**
Chapter 6:	What Does a Man of Significance Look Like?	**43**
Chapter 7:	Zeal and Discouragement	**55**
Chapter 8:	Just a Little More	**63**
Chapter 9:	Making a Real Difference	**71**
Chapter 10:	Coping with Discouragement and Fear	**81**
Chapter 11:	What Makes Me Me	**90**
Chapter 12:	It's Time to Jump	**100**

Chapter 13: Making a Plan   **108**

Chapter 14: Crossing the Finish Line   **119**

Chapter 15: The Finish Line   **131**

Epilogue   **139**

Acknowledgments   **140**

Notes   **141**

About the Author   **144**

Resources Available   **145**

INTRODUCTION

*"Let us focus upon doing what is important
rather than trying to be important."*

—Jim Grassi

As I celebrated yet another birthday, I launched into this work. My mind continues to hope that I could one day be in the NFL, or fly into space, or bench-press two hundred pounds—but my body and reality suggest that those dreams need to be buried. All I need to do is look in the mirror or listen to my grandchildren to realize that I'm on the shadow side of the mountain. Has my life been successful, significant, and a model of Christ?

Charles Dickens began *A Tale of Two Cities* with these memorable words: "It was the best of times, it was the worst of times . . . ."[1] I recall one of the best and worst years of my life. In 1981, I was a rising star as a deputy town manager. I had just received two awards for my leadership abilities. Through my bass fishing accomplishments, I was voted the top fisherman on the West Coast. I was writing for three different sports magazines. I was also a rising star in the fishing and hunting world as a competitive fisherman and co-host of a West Coast fishing program on television. A local university had me teaching one or two classes a semester. I had the perfect wife (my high school sweetheart) with two very gifted twin boys.

My spiritual life consisted of going to church, being in a Bible study group, meeting with a group of guys, and trying to be a godly role model at home, at work, and in my community. I endeavored to be a Spirit-filled man, but my flesh was weak and I failed in relationships because I became impatient with people. I had been involved in forming an organization called Let's Go Fishing Ministries, and subsequently had been asked to share our vision for discipleship at one of the largest Christian conference centers in the west.

My goal of being successful and important was within reach. I was living the American dream of being recognized as a successful person. After all, that was the message I heard almost every day from my father. He grew up during the Great Depression and never had the opportunity to go to college and, in his mind, being a bread driver wasn't a successful career. I regularly received the message from those adults around me: "Jimmy, make something of yourself." I was the first-born male of the family and it was clear that I was expected to make the best of my skills and abilities. I thought it would really be tough to beat the year I was having at the beginning of 1981. So I thought.

That winter was cold and damp, and it offered plenty of time to become introspective, especially about my health. For a few years, I had been having some heart issues. After going to three cardiologists who did all kinds of testing, I was told, "Jim, your only problem is that you are overly stressed and too busy. You are trying to put twenty gallons of stuff into a ten-gallon bucket." Instead of thinking about better balancing my life or restricting what I was doing, I asked the doctors for a tranquillizer to help me better cope with my out-of-control appetite for success. "Don't tell me not to burn the candle at both ends," I told the doctors. "Tell me where I can get more wax." I could blame my drivenness on upbringing or culture or the challenging childhood I had, but the reality was that the stress-filled life I was living was centered upon my workaholic nature, and it was up to me to find the peace of God—the one He speaks of in His Word (Phil. 4:7).

At a routine physical in February 1981, I continued to complain about my heart and blood pressure issue. The doctor asked if I had any other problems. I said, "I still have the ringing in my right ear." Ringing in an ear is about as common as a cold. He said, "More than likely it's nothing to worry about because we checked it out before, but to be safe, let's check it again." The young ear, nose, and throat doctor saw me as an experiment. He ordered up a batch of tests—the results of which started a journey to the "worst of times." After a month of continued testing, it was determined that I had a non-malignant brain tumor called an acoustic neuroma. Surgery was required.

The day finally arrived for the journey to the hospital. My dad had the car running in front of my house to take me to the hospital so that I would be ready for the early morning surgery the next day. I walked through the house one last time. The doctors said that the operation was very touchy as the tumor rested against my brainstem right at the place that controls my heart and blood pressure. As I walked into my study, I surveyed all my awards, trophies, degrees, and pictures that represented my rewards for the journey I had traveled thus far. In my mind's eye, all I could see were piles of dust. As Solomon observed, "I have seen all the works that are done under the sun; and indeed, all is vanity and grasping for the wind" (Eccl. 1:14). As I walked to the waiting car, I hugged my wife and young boys for what I thought could be the final time. Their warm tears against my cheek caused me to think about the real issues in life. When death is at your doorstep, only two things are important: your eternal security (believing in Jesus as your Savior) and the relationship you have with those you love and might leave behind.

That night while sitting in the sterile white hospital room, with no personal possessions to remind me of what I had achieved, I started to consider the depth of my faith and the regrets I had about not spending more time knowing God and making Him known. Oh, there had been moments with my wife and kids, but nothing like I would like to have had. There was always more to do, more things to get, more to take up the creative energies of my efforts, and of course the worn-out phrase, "I'm just too busy." As I endeavored to try and get some sleep, my tears of regret began to dampen my pillow. I knew then that if I survived the surgery, life would have to be different in the future. I saw in our twin sons the gifts God had given them and knew I wanted to be there to encourage and support them as they developed their own careers and families. My loyal and dedicated wife needed a husband who would love her and be devoted to enriching her life.

The nine-and-a-half-hour surgery left me with temporary facial paralysis on my right side, vision problems, no hearing in my right ear, and a loss of balance. I became dependent upon therapy and drugs. During my three-week hospital stay and a second surgery, God kept drumming into my heart the same message He gave the apostle Paul:

> But if I live on in the flesh, this will mean fruit from my labor; yet what I shall choose I cannot tell. For I am hard-pressed between the two, having a desire to depart and be with Christ, which is far better. Nevertheless to remain in the flesh is more needful for you.

And being confident of this, I know that I shall remain and continue with you all for your progress and joy of faith, that your rejoicing for me may be more abundant in Jesus Christ by my coming to you again." (Phil. 1:22–26)

If you recall one of the final scenes of the film *Saving Private Ryan*, Captain John Miller's squad from Company C of the 2nd Ranger Battalion was fighting to save a little village called Ramelle. Captain Miller, played by Tom Hanks, lay mortally wounded on the east side of the bridge. The Germans were finally being pushed back by American planes and troops as he took his final moments to express his feelings to Private James Ryan. As he looked up into the eyes of Private Ryan, the sole remaining son to carry on his family name, Captain Miller said, "James, earn this . . . earn it."[2] What Captain Miller was reminding all of us is to make our lives count!

Every time I see that movie and come to the last scene, I think back on the days of recovery from my surgery and think about my life being one that is spent on the right priorities. God did more than a life-saving surgery in the hospital; He transplanted into my heart the desire to make my life count, to trust and serve Him to the best of my abilities for the rest of my life. I don't believe that every person who is getting his life priorities straight should go into full-time ministry. It is a calling from God upon the heart, an anointed appointment. Just as some are born and gifted to be musicians, artists, and so forth, a person who is called and equipped by God is doing what he feels led to do.

Some of the most effective men I know are in business or the trades and impact people for Jesus where they are. For me at that particular time, the lesson learned was more about how I go about my daily tasks of being an effective administrator/businessman. Scripture tells us to abide in Christ and bear much fruit (John 15:2, 5). I now had a new standard to measure my progress and success. Was I doing things just to exalt myself, or was there going to be a deeper and more profound meaning to my work? Was I going to squander my time watching television or just hanging out, or would I use my life to do something that had eternal consequences?

In our culture, too many people have an "entitlement" mentality. The idea that we should work hard at what we do as honoring to our Lord doesn't seem to resonate with most people. What I share in this book may seem a little foreign to people who are sitting on the sidelines of life hoping the world will change. My friend, you and I are the change agents. We need a fresh understanding of God's plan for our lives and the purpose for which He created us. If ever there was a time we needed to be modeling a life of success and significance to the future generations, it is now!

As we consider how we go about switching from a life pursuing success to doing things that have eternal significance, we will discover biblical truths that will transform us into more balanced and Christ-centered people. Whether you are twenty or ninety, the one question you must ask is, how will *you* live out the remainder of your life? God calls each one of us to finish well and finish strong.

In his masterful book *A Life Well Lived*, Pastor Chuck Swindoll tells us, "In those best/worst seasons of life, when the cold of winter prunes us back to the stump, we can do little more than mourn our losses, cling to an uncertain hope of spring, and allow God to strengthen our roots."[3] It is my prayer that, as you read through this book, you will find a better balanced life that helps you understand the eternal and internal blessings received from being obedient to God's plan for your life. As we consider portions of God's Word on this important topic, we'll discover new truths that will help us on life's journey. It is my prayer that the moments you invest in finishing well and finishing strong will bring you to a new sense of understanding and awareness of the joy-filled life God has for you.

Paul endeavored to inspire the young Timothy with advice about praying for those we love:

> Therefore I exhort first of all that supplications, prayers, intercessions, and giving of thanks be made for all men, for kings and all who are in authority, that we may lead a quiet and peaceable life in all godliness and reverence. For this is good and acceptable in the sight of God our Savior, who desires all men to be saved and to come to the knowledge of the truth. (1 Tim. 2:1–4)

"Every person must decide whether to walk in the light of creative altruism or in the darkness of destructive selfishness. This is the judgment. Life's most urgent question is, what are you doing for others?"

—**Dr. Martin Luther King Jr.**[1]

WHAT IT MEANS
TO FINISH
WELL AND STRONG

What does it mean to finish well and finish strong? First of all, the concept of "finishing" refers to a man's entire life. It addresses the question, "What will I be remembered for after I'm gone?" And that's primarily what this entire book is concerned with—helping men, especially young men, to live their lives with deliberate purpose, working constantly toward a goal of being able to look back one day on a life well lived.

The concept of "finishing" can also be seen in things like running in a race. An Olympic marathon runner is an amazing athlete, able to make his body do things that most of us could only dream of doing, but his running is of little value if he doesn't actually cross the finish line. A man who runs lightning fast for two miles then drops out of the race will never win a gold medal. So first and foremost we should understand that the Christian life is concerned, at least in part, not merely with running but with *finishing*. Life is not a sprint but a marathon.

Yet that is not the whole picture; we are not merely concerned with finishing, but with finishing *well* and *strong*. A few years back, a woman made national news when she won the women's division in the Boston Marathon, setting some new records—only to be revealed as a fraud. It turned out that she had not run in the race at all, merely jumping out of the crowd near the finish line and pretending to have

1

done the entire 26.2 miles. She might have crossed the finish line, but she did not do it well.

BASIC DEFINITIONS

Let's begin by getting some basic definitions for our terms. Both words, of course, can be used in a variety of ways to mean different things, but we'll concern ourselves only with the words as they apply to becoming a godly man who finishes *well* and *strong*.

FINISHING WELL

The dictionary defines *well* to mean "in accordance with a good or high standard of conduct or morality."[2] There's a subtle distinction here from the way that we frequently use the word in conversation, and we'll need to understand this distinction right up front. We might say, "John did well in the race," meaning that John got a better time than other runners or finished ahead of them. But that use of the word *well* is a relative one—that is, he did well *in relation to* or comparison with other people.

But our concept of *finishing life well* does not mean "finishing life better than others did." As you read through this book, you'll realize that finishing one's life better in some ways than others is precisely the way the world measures success, but that isn't the way God measures success. God's definition of a life *lived well* is to compare it with His own standard of success, which was established by His Son, Jesus. We'll discuss this more in a moment, but it's important to understand right from the beginning: to *live well* is to live the way that Jesus lived.

The dictionary also defines *well* as "carefully, attentively," "in a thorough manner." We use the word this way when we say, "John built that bookcase very well." He made the bookcase carefully, paying attention to fine details and making it thoroughly solid. This, too, is an aspect of living well—to pay attention to the little details of living like Christ, and striving to be like Him thoroughly, covering every area of our lives. And again, that's what this book is all about: *to help us understand what it means to live like Jesus, and to see the practical, day-to-day ways that we can thoroughly imitate His model.*

Thus the words *finishing well* as used in this book will actually relate to the daily tasks and challenges God puts before us. We as disciples should work unto our master as unto the Lord. We take on our jobs, responsibilities, and tasks with a sense that we are representing our Lord in whatever we do and that our job is to demonstrate the joy, love, peace, and wisdom of Christ within us.

FINISHING STRONG

When I speak about *finishing strong*, I'm not concerned with physical power, like that of a professional football player. Samson was one of the strongest men in history in physical terms, yet his life is not a good example of what it means to "finish strong." The dictionary helps us understand the type of strength that we're concerned about: "having great moral power of endurance or effort; firm in will or purpose; brave, courageous, resolute."

In this work, *finishing strong* refers to the way we apply ourselves to ending the journey. We set a vision and expectation for ourselves that suggests we aren't going to go to the bench after we retire, but instead want to be in the game of helping change lives. Our goal for our lives has eternal significance that isn't limited to when we get a social security check or reach a certain financial level of comfort or accumulate enough stuff to be recognized or have the power and prestige that suggest we are important. Our focus needs to be placed on *doing what is important* rather than *being important*.

Let's return to the example of a man running a race. A sprinter just needs to be fast. The gun fires, the runners take off, and a few seconds later the race is over. But the marathon runner needs something different: he needs endurance, devotion, stamina, and a vision to finish strong even though he can't see the finish line from the start. In fact, a marathon champion might not be nearly as quick as a sprinting champion, because his focus is on the long-haul, not the short run. He needs to pace himself carefully, keeping in mind with every step that he needs to hang in for a full 26.2 miles.

The same is true for the Christian life. We are in this for the long-haul, not for the short sprint. It's relatively easy to do a Christlike deed from time to time, to overlook an offense, to write a check on

Sunday morning, or resist an occasional temptation. But God calls His people to let the character of Christ permeate every fiber of our being, coming back to the concept of being "thorough" in our lives. This means that growing in strength requires us to grow in *perseverance*, to gain the quality of hanging in the race even when it's all uphill for a long stretch.

And there are times when life will require real endurance and perseverance. Paul used the metaphor of a boxer's endurance when he said, "Thus I fight: not as one who beats the air. But I discipline my body and bring it into subjection, lest, when I have preached to others, I myself should become disqualified" (1 Cor. 9:26–27). We are not fighting "as one who beats the air," as Paul put it—that is, one who "shadow boxes" or swings his fists just for exercise. Rather, we are engaged in a genuine warfare against two foes: against the devil and his minions, who work ceaselessly to destroy souls; and against our own flesh. And neither of these foes ever gets tired of trying to lure us away from God's Word.

Steve Farrar, in his epic work *Finishing Strong*, wrote, "It is the teachable man who finishes strong."[3] Being teachable is the key to finishing well and strong, because there is always more to learn about becoming like Christ. Sadly, as we grow older we generally become less and less teachable, so it is important for a man to develop a habit early in life of being willing to change and to learn.

SOME EXAMPLES FROM SCRIPTURE

The best way to learn how to be a godly man is to imitate one, and the Bible is the logical place to start looking for such examples. Let's consider just a few of the great men and women who demonstrated what it means to finish well and strong.

JESUS

The Bible tells us that Jesus "has done all things well" (Mark 7:37). He is the perfect example of what it means to finish well and strong. Indeed, He is the very *definition* of that concept! To live life well and strong means to live as Christ lived. He obeyed the Father in all things;

He gave His very life in order that others might live; He endured and persevered even though the whole world was set against Him.

It is worth noting here that, by the world's standards, Jesus' life was a failure. Jesus became a man in order to remove the curse of sin and death that had reigned in mankind since Adam—yet He ended His ministry by dying Himself. He was the Messiah, the Holy One sent from God to bring peace to the human race—yet He was executed like a worthless criminal. From the perspective of the people around Him, it looked like He failed completely in His mission. Sometimes finishing well and strong in God's eyes will look like waste and failure in man's eyes.

THE APOSTLE PAUL

Paul spent his younger years as a Pharisee, pursuing what he thought was an eternal goal through legalism and violence. But when he met Christ on the road to Damascus, he learned that the only way to store up eternal treasure is through the blood of Jesus, which He shed on the cross.

The interesting thing about Paul is that he demonstrated how a man can change his goals and pursuits midlife and still finish well and strong. Paul was not being boastful when he stated, "I have fought the good fight, I have finished the race, I have kept the faith" (2 Tim. 4:7). He was merely stating a fact, showing us that the goal is readily attainable, regardless how a man has lived in the past.

DAVID

David was a man's man. When he was young, he slew both a lion and a bear single-handedly. He killed a giant in battle, despite having never fought in combat before—and using just a sling against a foe encased in armor. In later life, he led an army to victory against his nation's deadly enemies. He rose to become king of one of the world's superpowers in his day. He also wrote poetry, leaving a legacy of psalms that are still read and sung worldwide today, thousands of years later.

Yet he was not without flaws. He committed adultery, then murdered the woman's husband to avoid being caught. He did not discipline his sons effectively, and watched as one of his sons plunged his nation into civil war. Nevertheless, he was described as a man after God's own heart (1 Sam. 13:14), and he finished his life well and strong.

SAMSON

Samson is an example of a man who did not live a godly life. He was gifted with tremendous physical strength and had the potential to do great things in God's service. But his physical strength was not coupled with self-control or discipline, and he squandered his gifts in pursuit of physical indulgence. Nevertheless, God in His grace continued to give Samson opportunities to repent and devote himself to His service, and at the very end of his life he did so. He is listed as one of the heroes of the faith in Hebrews 11, demonstrating that God can salvage even the most wasted life.

SOME MORE EXAMPLES

HUDSON TAYLOR

James Hudson Taylor committed his life to Christ after reading a tract at age seventeen. Very soon after, he became convicted that God wanted him to journey to China to spread the gospel, even though he had no knowledge of Chinese customs or languages. Nevertheless, he spent several years learning Mandarin Chinese, as well as Greek and Hebrew, and studying medicine to prepare himself for the task of ministering in China.

Taylor devoted his entire adult life to serving the people of China, preaching the gospel and providing medical aid to a nation that, at times, didn't want it. He suffered through riots, civil war, robbery, fires, and much more hardship. He watched several of his children die young, and lost his wife to cholera. He endured much suffering and sorrow, yet he was committed to doing the Lord's work in China and establishing what is today known as the China Inland Mission.

WILLIAM WILBERFORCE

William Wilberforce lived in England during a time when slavery was an accepted fact of life. He was from a wealthy family, had become a member of Parliament, and enjoyed an indulgent and somewhat luxurious lifestyle. But in his mid twenties, he began reading the Bible and was challenged to dedicate his life to Christ. He quickly realized that he needed to be like Christ in all areas of his life, and this included his involvement in Parliament and British politics.

It wasn't long after this that Wilberforce became convicted that slavery needed to be abolished. He worked tirelessly throughout his adult life to eradicate slavery and to spread the gospel, both at home and abroad, but the full abolition of slavery did not come to England until shortly after Wilberforce had died.

JIM ELLIOT

Jim Elliot grew up in a Christian home in Oregon and dedicated his life to Christ at an early age. During his time in college, he developed a deep interest in foreign missions, considering that his highest calling in life was to spread the gospel to people who had never heard of Jesus. He felt led to Ecuador to bring the Bible and gospel deep in the jungles to an indigenous group known at the time as the Auca.

But when Jim and his four co-missionaries arrived to take up new lives in Ecuador, they were met by a group of Auca warriors, who almost immediately speared them all to death. Jim had recently married his college sweetheart Elisabeth, and his death seemed like a tragic waste at the time. But Elisabeth returned to the Auca people some years later, determined to fulfill her late husband's calling of bringing the gospel into the jungles. As a result, many of the very men who murdered Jim Elliot and his friends came to Christ. As Jim wrote in his journal, "He is no fool who gives what he cannot keep to gain that which he cannot lose.[4]

PERSONAL ACTIVITIES

During the coming month, read a biography of a Christian who finished well and strong. You can choose one of the men listed above or ask your mentoring partner for recommendations. What aspects of his or her life inspired you? In what sense did the person finish well and strong? In what ways might you imitate his or her example?

MENTORING ACTIVITIES

Choose one of the following men, and spend time together with your mentoring partner studying his life. In what sense did that man finish well and strong? How did he accomplish this? What did it cost him?

✳ Paul

✳ Samuel

✳ David

✳ Moses

✳ Joseph

START WELL
TO FINISH WELL

Daniel was a young man, probably a teenager, living in Jerusalem during the reign of King Jehoiakim. He was good-looking and intelligent, both quick-witted and quick to learn. He might also have been of noble birth, with connections to the king's court. He was, in short, a young man with great potential and a bright future before him. Daniel was poised to be a successful man by the world's standards.

Then the Babylonian army invaded his homeland and carried him away as a slave. Success was no longer the goal; now it was survival. Daniel's tragedy is the sort of event that would make most young men become bitter and despondent. But in addition to the many qualities that Daniel demonstrated, his greatest was also his most important: he had wisdom. He did not give in to despair, nor did he become angry that God had somehow abandoned him or betrayed him. Instead, he made a firm resolution that he would remain obedient to God's Word, despite the fact that circumstances had taken such a horrible turn.

The reason we know these details of Daniel's life and character is that, shortly after carrying them off to Babylon, King Nebuchadnezzar selected some of the young men from Israel to serve in his court, "some of the children of Israel and some of the king's descendants and some of the nobles, young men in whom there was no blemish, but good-looking, gifted in all wisdom, possessing knowledge and quick to understand, who had ability to serve in the king's palace, and whom they might teach the language and literature of the Chaldeans" (Dan. 1:3–4). Despite being carried into slavery by an enemy nation, Daniel knew that God was still completely in control of all events.

Daniel was a man who finished well, holding high offices in the courts of three successive kings in Babylon and Persia, and writing an important book of prophecy that became part of the Old Testament. One reason that he finished well, however, was that he *started* well by determining while he was young how he would spend his life until he was old. As soon as he was appointed to the court of King Nebuchadnezzar, Daniel found himself faced with a difficult decision. The king determined what Daniel and his peers should eat, since they were to become important members of his court, and this diet included food that violated Daniel's conscience. We are not told the specifics, but the king's diet probably included food that had been sacrificed to idols, as well as meat that God had declared unclean (Lev. 11; Deut. 14).

Daniel's response to this situation is revealing. "But Daniel purposed in his heart that he would not defile himself" (Dan. 1:8). The Hebrew word translated "purposed" simply means "he put it" in his heart. In other words, Daniel made a deliberate decision not to defile himself before God, and he placed it in his heart like granite, a solid rock of determination on which he would gradually build his whole life.

SUCCESS OR SIGNIFICANCE?

Daniel was an unusual young man. Most of us spend our youth differently than he did—of course, most of us also aren't carried away as slaves into a foreign land. But for most of us, our youthful years are spent laying a groundwork for the future in terms of success in the things of this world. We are eager to finish high school so that we can get to college or begin working for "real money." We spend our college years longing for graduation and beginning a career. We meet the woman of our dreams and settle down—and our focus shifts to climbing the corporate ladder in order to better provide for the growing family.

In other words, a young man's mind-set is nearly always consumed with thoughts of the future. The problem is that most of us focus on the wrong future, looking ahead to the time we have remaining in our lives and anticipating the needs of this world. Daniel, by contrast, was focused on his *eternal* future, anticipating when he was young what he wanted to become—not when he was old, but when he was in eternity.

A young man tends to be driven, to be motivated by forces within himself that demand success. As he gets older, his drive shifts in a subtle way, and he begins to strive for significance, wanting not merely to succeed in his pursuits, but to have those pursuits be meaningful in some way. This is the beginning of a wise focus, this desire to invest oneself into work that has lasting meaning: meaning that lasts not for a lifetime, but forever.

I was speaking at a conference a few years back that was attended by a large group of young men, mostly in their twenties or early thirties. I opened a time for questions near the end, and one young man instantly raised his hand. His question took me by surprise. "We're just getting started in life," he said, "and we want to start out right. How can we *start* right so that we *finish* right?"

Needless to say, I was delighted by this young man's insight, because he had put his finger directly on the key to becoming a man of God: to *finish* well, at some point a man needs to *start* well. When we're young, we're tempted to live on an adrenaline rush, pumped by the thrill of risk, energized by wheeling and dealing, hungry for adventure. We can even become addicted, so to speak, to the risk of the unknown, to acquiring power or authority, to the greed and pride that temporarily give us a sort of high.

But the irony is that it is very common for men in their retirement years to look back on a life characterized by boredom. This seems like a paradox, after spending one's youth in pursuit of adventure. But that is just it: it's merely a pursuit, and the rare occasions when a man attains that adrenaline rush prove to be fleeting moments. Many older men lament a life spent with too much television, too little exercise; too many lone-wolf pursuits and too little participation with family and the work of God's kingdom.

The important element in Daniel's example was not his youth, but his determination. It is best, of course, for a man to make a determination for godliness when he is young, but it is never too late. Indeed, the best time to purpose in one's heart to obey God is now, to reestablish that commitment on a daily basis. And, in my own experience, that commitment does need to be reestablished regularly, because the cares of life and the pressures of the world are constantly eating away at it, like water against a rock.

How do we stop this erosion process? The things of the world are contrary to the things of God, and it is those forces that will make it most difficult to maintain a firm purpose in our hearts toward obedience. The apostle John tells us, "Do not love the world or the things in the world. If anyone loves the world, the love of the Father is not in him. For all that is in the world—the lust of the flesh, the lust of the eyes, and the pride of life—is not of the Father but is of the world" (1 John 2:15–16). These three areas of sin—lust of the flesh, lust of the eyes, and the pride of life—are traps that the world uses to short-circuit our resolves to obey God. Let's consider each of these areas in more detail.

LUST OF THE FLESH

The phrase "lust of the flesh" certainly includes improper sexual activity, but it is not limited to that. John was speaking of anything that caters to physical appetites and cravings. Let's consider a few areas of fleshly lust as examples, remembering that this is by no means a complete list of potential pitfalls.

SEXUAL IMMORALITY

God intended the sexual union to take place only within the confines of marriage. Therefore, any sexual activity that takes place outside of a marital relationship is contrary to God's will. And this includes more than actual intercourse with another person. Jesus said that lustful thoughts are the same as committing adultery (Matt. 5:28), which means that looking at pornography is included in the category of sexual immorality.

Take practical steps to strengthen your resolve in this area. Shun pornography at all times. Avoid social websites that lack accountability, which might lead to inappropriate relationships—whether real or merely "virtual." Stand guard at all times to prevent any relationship from becoming inappropriately intimate, such as with a married woman or, if you're single, with a non-Christian, whether married or otherwise.

Our culture bombards us with sexual images; a man cannot buy groceries or even drive down the freeway without seeing seductive advertising. And these images come at us when we are not looking for them; how much worse, then, to put yourself in a place where you know in advance that you will be tempted. Do everything you can, at all times, consciously and deliberately, to avoid situations and settings where the devil can gain a sexual foothold in your mind.

GLUTTONY AND DRUNKENNESS

An area of struggle that Christians rarely discuss is that of gluttony, yet it is a form of "lust of the flesh," a way in which we fall into the trap of indulging the flesh. And whatever your view of a Christian's use of alcohol, there is no question that drunkenness is a sin (Eph. 5:18).

Yet gluttony is not exhibited only in eating great quantities of food. A man who refuses to eat something that he considers "second-rate" is in danger of becoming a glutton. A man who drinks wine with dinner might not be a drunkard; but a man who insists on only the best wine might well be a glutton. The issue is not with what we eat or how much, but with our attitude toward food and drink. It's easy to make eating an increasingly high priority in our lives, until it becomes like a god.

Take practical steps to strengthen your resolve in this area. Try scheduling a partial fast once a week for a month, skipping one meal and spending that time in prayer or Bible study. (This, too, can become a trap, incidentally, making a man legalistic or self-righteous—which is why I suggest trying this just for a limited time.) Make it a point to give the choice selections to others when not dining alone. And always stop to give thanks for God's provision prior to eating, bowing your head and focusing on being thankful, even if you're dining in public.

LAZINESS AND SELF-INDULGENCE

Another common trap of indulging one's flesh involves our use of time and resources. Our culture urges us to spend our time in the pursuit of pleasure, striving to gain more free time so that we can spend it on ourselves. We tend to grow lazy in areas involving self-discipline, not because we are naturally inclined to lie on the sofa, but because we are more focused on spending our energies having fun.

Take practical steps to strengthen your resolve in this area. Make it a point once a week to voluntarily give up a block of free time that you might have spent on hobbies or leisure, and spend it instead on serving someone. At all times, be willing to drop what you're doing in order to serve your own family, spending time with wife and kids, or helping someone from church.

LUST OF THE EYES

Lust of the eyes is similar to lust of the flesh in that it involves feeding our human appetites. But it differs in that lust of the eyes is a bit more subtle than lust of the flesh. It's easy to recognize that it's wrong to lust for a woman, but it's sometimes more difficult to recognize covetousness or greed. We tend to justify these sins by convincing ourselves that we have a genuine need or by rationalizing that we'll be saving time and money in the long run if we acquire some material thing today.

Once again, our culture pressures us to be covetous, bombarding us with advertising, urging us to buy things that we might never have thought of owning otherwise. The world of technology is like a powerful drug, always making us crave more; the day you buy the newest cell phone gadget, someone comes out with a new upgrade with more features and power. The lust of the eyes is a never-ending downward spiral—a lust that is never satisfied. "Turn away my eyes from looking at worthless things," the psalmist cried, "and revive me in Your way" (Ps. 119:37).

One dire consequence of the lust of the eyes is that we become ungrateful for the blessings that God has poured out in our lives. Our eyes see something shiny and new, and we become dissatisfied with the tarnished old things that we already have. In this sense, the opposite of lust of the eyes is contentment—and contentment is a conscious choice, not a condition that comes upon us from external circumstances.

Take practical steps to strengthen your resolve in this area. Deliberately spend time every day giving thanks to God. When something in your life starts giving you trouble, turn away from the tendency to think about replacing it with something new and turn your thoughts to giving thanks for all the things that are going well in your life.

PRIDE OF LIFE

The pride of life is perhaps the most subtle of the three areas of sin that John lists in this verse (1 John 2:16). The phrase refers to numerous pitfalls, including materialism, a desire for luxury, a longing for the nicest things, a dissatisfaction with "good enough" things, and so forth. It can also refer to a desire for praise and honor, for recognition from others for things we've accomplished.

Yet I think there is a type of pride of life that is even more subtle than these things. It is natural for a man to strive for success, to want to gain mastery in whatever he undertakes. This is the way God made us, and it is a good thing to aim for excellence in all that we do. But this, too, can become a trap, and there is a subtle point at which our striving for excellence can degenerate into the pride of life.

Pride of life can refer to a yearning for success or excellence or mastery for its own sake; it becomes a matter of pride to a man to excel beyond his peers. He strives to go beyond everyone else, not because he is doing it to please God, but because it pleases himself, because it is a matter of pride.

Take practical steps to strengthen your resolve in this area. Cultivate a mind-set in which you picture yourself doing something in direct service to God. If you mow the lawn, for example, picture yourself mowing the front lawn at Jesus' house. When you are at work, picture yourself doing your daily job, whatever it might be, with Jesus as your supervisor. Remember Paul's admonition: "And whatever you do, do it heartily, as to the Lord and not to men, knowing that from the Lord you will receive the reward of the inheritance; for you serve the Lord Christ" (Col. 3:23–24).

ACCOUNTABILITY

In all these areas of struggle, an important key is to be in an accountability group—and that's what mentoring partnerships are for! One of the essential ingredients in your mentoring sessions together is to have an accountability time, when each man asks direct questions concerning areas of personal struggle. "Have you looked at pornography this past week?" "What's going on in your relationship with so-and-so?" "How have you been spending your free time recently?"

Make accountability a nonnegotiable aspect of your mentoring relationship. If your time together is limited, there are several things that you should make top priorities: prayer, Bible study, and accountability. Complete honesty and transparency are also imperatives in the mentoring partnership, and both of you need to be willing to share what areas you're struggling in. You'll be surprised, as a general rule, to discover that your partner has struggled in the same area.

PERSONAL ACTIVITIES

Spend time this week reflecting on Paul's statement: "Not that I have already attained, or am already perfected; but I press on, that I may lay hold of that for which Christ Jesus has also laid hold of me" (Phil. 3:12). Come to your mentoring time prepared to discuss this passage. What does it mean to "press on"? For what purpose did Jesus lay hold of you?

MENTORING ACTIVITIES

Spend time together discussing Paul's words in Philippians 3 that you meditated on individually. Why did God "lay hold" of each of you? What reasons might He have in bringing you together as mentoring partners?

Discuss areas where each of you desire accountability, then agree on how you will do so for each other. How often will you "check in" with each other on those topics? What goals do you hope to attain?

"The quality, not the longevity, of one's life is what is important."
—**Dr. Martin Luther King Jr.**[1]

THE DASH ON MY TOMBSTONE

Ted was a very talented young man, a friend of mine from the days when we were both young and had grand aspirations. He was deeply committed to God and family, beginning a promising career as an engineer and heavily involved in ministry at our church. When we got to know each other, he had just become engaged to be married to Michelle, a beautiful woman he'd met in high school youth group.

Ted and Michelle were married and bought a nice home near our church; time went along, and our spheres of work and ministry caused us to lose touch for a time. Then one day, a few years later, I learned that Ted had been diagnosed with a rare form of cancer—and that began an extended period of slow decline for him, as he gradually succumbed to his deadly illness.

That illness lasted for several years, years of pain and increasing levels of debilitation for Ted, and Michelle found it a hard burden to care for him and earn a living. In time, she met someone else and divorced Ted, leaving him alone and stranded without income or health care. His health continued to decline, perhaps accelerated by heartbreak, and in the end he died in his mid-thirties.

This is a tragic story, and one might be tempted to think that this promising life was wasted. Ted did not have any children to carry on his name. There are no monuments to him, no scholarship funds in his honor, no public buildings or streets named after him. He had so much potential, great skill in his chosen area of work, a lovely wife, a strong Christian family and church to support him, but he was "cut down" in the prime of his life.

Yet that way of thinking is not God's way of thinking. The truth is that Ted did leave a legacy behind as an example of faithfulness during times of hardship. It's been years now since he died, but people still talk about the things that he said and did during his terminal illness. Just the other day, I overheard two friends at church discussing the concept of God's sovereignty in our lives, and one of them said, "I remember the time that Ted told me that God is in control over all events, even the tough ones. And he knew what he was talking about!"

Ted's story was not the sort of thing that anyone would choose, of course. It certainly wasn't what he would have chosen. But we don't get to choose the circumstances of our lives, and most people would not choose *any* form of suffering if given the opportunity. As the author of Hebrews wrote, "No discipline seems pleasant at the time, but painful. Later on, however, it produces a harvest of righteousness and peace for those who have been trained by it" (Heb. 12:11 NIV).

We don't get to choose the circumstances in our lives, but we do get to choose how we will respond in those circumstances. In large measure, we determine how we will be remembered after we're gone from this world. The important thing is not to live long but to live well. We need to focus not on the dates of our tombstone, but on the dash in between those dates, on the person we become rather than the successes we attain. Our focus should be on *significance* rather than *success.*

WRITING YOUR OWN EPITAPH

It might sound morbid to be talking about what will be written on your gravestone after you die, but it is a very important topic that demands attention. You've probably heard the famous Latin phrase *carpe diem,* meaning "seize the day." This is the motto of our modern American culture, the notion of "look out for number one," take what you want, don't be satisfied with what you have but crave more.

But here's another Latin phrase that is more important to understand: *memento mori.* It's probably one you've never encountered before, yet my parents' generation were all very familiar with it. It means "remember that you will die." This phrase originated in ancient Rome, where a victorious general would be given a parade after defeating an enemy army in battle. The general would be carried through Rome in his chariot with great splendor and fanfare—but behind him in the chariot stood a slave whose job it was to whisper in his ear, *"Memento mori*—today you are a victorious leader, but one day you will die." This fact is an absolute certainty for all of us as a result of Adam's sin, and because of that sin God told Adam, "In the sweat of your face you shall eat bread till you return to the ground, for out of it you were taken; for dust you are, and to dust you shall return" (Gen. 3:19).

My friend Ted understood this concept in a very real sense when he was diagnosed with a terminal illness. The reality of his mortality was driven home to him the day that a doctor told him that his death was imminent. In that moment, Ted came to realize that he had a limited time left in which to create a lasting legacy with his life. This truth applies to each of us; it's just that most of us don't know in advance when our lives will end.

The key, then, is to live our lives with the full realization that our days are numbered, making every day count in service to God. What we need to remember is that it isn't when you were born or when you died that people remember—it's that dash in between. We need to remind ourselves at all times that "our citizenship is in heaven" (Phil. 3:20), that we are not citizens of this world, and we do not want to waste time pursuing the things of this world.

Paul warned the Philippian Christians that they must never set their minds on earthly things. Those who pursue earthly goals end up making their bellies their gods, using all their energies and resources serving their flesh—and, as we discussed in chapter 1, this is a root of great sin. Paul, in fact, states that such people become the enemy of God. "For many walk, of whom I have told you often, and now tell you even weeping, that they are the enemies of the cross of Christ: whose end is destruction, whose god is their belly, and whose glory is in their shame—who set their mind on earthly things" (Phil. 3:18–19).

Let's consider two examples from the Bible of men whose lives illustrated these principles. One man demonstrated what happens when we set our mind on the flesh; one demonstrated what it means to set our mind on the spirit.

THE EXAMPLE OF BALAAM

Let's first consider the life of someone who set his mind on earthly things. When the Israelites were making their way from Egypt to the promised land, they passed through the territory that belonged to the Moabites. Balak, the king of the Moabites, became afraid and hired a man named Balaam to put a curse on the people of Israel. (The complete story can be found in Numbers 22–25.)

Balaam was a famous sorcerer in that day, dealing in the occult, something that is absolutely forbidden for God's people. But we are going to look at another aspect of his life which concerns us here, the fact that he placed a higher priority on material gain than he did on obedience to the Word of God.

King Balak sent some of his important cabinet members to speak with Balaam, asking him to put a curse on the people of Israel, delivering a large payment in advance with the potential for more once he had completed his evil task. Rather than refusing outright to do something that was clearly wrong, Balaam asked God whether or not to accept the offer. God told him that He had blessed the people of Israel, and anyone who attempted to curse them would himself be cursed instead. Yet Balaam disregarded God's commands and went with the men to put a curse on Israel.

Now God showed much grace to Balaam along the way, repeatedly warning him not to attempt placing a curse on Israel. He even sent an angel to appear to Balaam, and opened the mouth of Balaam's donkey so that it could speak! But Balaam was captivated with the things of this world, and he was more concerned with worldly success than with obedience to God. He thought he could have things both ways, obeying God at a level that was convenient to him, while still making some money and gaining prestige as the king's personal soothsayer.

Jesus warned about the danger of this kind of thinking. "No one can serve two masters," He said, "for either he will hate the one and love the other, or else he will be loyal to the one and despise the other. You cannot serve God and mammon" (Matt. 6:24). Balaam demonstrated the truth of this in his life, and he ended up being an enemy of God and His people. The end result of Balaam's actions was that the men of Israel were led into sexual sins with the women of Midian, so Balaam's attempted compromise caused wickedness in the lives of others as well as himself.

Balaam did not leave a godly legacy; he did not finish well or strong.

THE EXAMPLE OF STEPHEN

Now let's turn to a more encouraging example of a man who set his mind on the things of God. We do not know a great deal about Stephen, other than that he was a Christian living in Jerusalem in the years following Jesus' resurrection and ascension to heaven—and we know the legacy he left behind. We don't know what he did to earn a living; we don't know whether he was wealthy or poor; we don't know what his gifts and talents were. We do know, however, that he had a good reputation among those who knew him, a reputation for being godly and consistent in his life. (Read Stephen's story in Acts 6–7.)

This is a good legacy already. The man who is consistent does not attempt to serve two masters, the way Balaam did. He is willing to sacrifice wealth and prestige in order to be fully sold out to God's will. The Word and will of God permeated Stephen's whole life, and there was no inconsistency between his words and his actions. This did not mean that he had no enemies; he developed some simply by preaching the gospel. But when those enemies wanted to arrest him, they could not find anything in his life to accuse him of—so they hired thugs to invent lies about him.

Stephen's life was characterized by the Spirit of God. His priorities and activities and the very words of his mouth were all centered on God's Word and eternal kingdom. This is the opposite of the man who is focused on the things of the flesh, which the Bible calls "a carnal man," meaning a "flesh-minded" man. Balaam was a flesh-minded man because his priority was to gain the things of this world. Remember that it is not possible to pursue the things of the world *and* the things of God; they are mutually exclusive.

And the man who pursues worldly gain makes himself God's enemy. Paul told the Christians in Rome that a person who sets his mind on worldly gain begins to make the flesh his god, in the sense of obeying the desires and cravings of his body, and this leads to death and enmity with God (Rom. 8:6–7). This is a very serious business!

YOUR GODLY LEGACY

Stephen's legacy was similar to that of my friend Ted who died young. His life was cut short by circumstances beyond his control, but he became an example and testimony to the people around him by the life he led. But this does not mean that a godly legacy can only come through suffering and hardship. On the contrary, your legacy is determined by how you live in all circumstances, the good times as well as the bad.

One very important way of leaving a good legacy is by raising godly children. They will learn how to be godly men and women by watching *you* being a godly man. This is actually just another application of the principle we are considering here, because your children will learn from your example just as my friends and I learned from the example of Ted, just as the people in Stephen's day learned from watching him as he gave his life as the church's first martyr.

Our culture is in desperate need of godly fathers. David Blankenhorn gave us some sobering facts in his book *Fatherless America*:

> This astonishing fact is reflected in many statistics, but here are the two most important. Tonight, about 40 percent of American children will go to sleep in homes in which their fathers do not live. Before they reach the age of eighteen, more than half of our nation's children are likely to spend at least a significant portion of their childhoods living apart from their fathers. Never before in this country have so many children been voluntarily abandoned by their fathers. Never before have so many children grown up without knowing what it means to have a father.[2]

But you can reverse this trend! Perhaps that is precisely what God is calling you to do—to be one of the godly men of your culture who raises a generation of godly, obedient Christian men and women. In fact, I'll go beyond this and say that, if you are a father, God most definitely *is* calling you to that task.

TEACHABLE *AND* OBEDIENT

In an earlier chapter, I mentioned the importance of having a teachable spirit. I want to reiterate this, as it is vitally important for a man to remain teachable throughout his lifetime. But there is another facet to this trait, and that is obedience. We do not develop a teachable spirit just for the sake of learning things. It is no good to learn something new if you never use it, and it is no good to learn the will of God if you don't *obey* it!

James tells us that the Word of God is like a mirror, and reading Scripture is like checking your reflection before you go to an important meeting. Suppose that you had an interview for a job or promotion that you really wanted. You look in the mirror and notice that you have spinach stuck in your teeth. What would you do?

Now imagine that you noticed the gross green stuff stuck in your teeth, shrugged your shoulders, straightened your tie—and walked into the interview with a big grin. Pretty dumb, right? But that is precisely what we do when we read God's Word, then shrug it off and get back to the "important" things in our lives. "For if anyone is a hearer of the word and not a doer," James tells us, "he is like a man observing his natural face in a mirror; for he observes himself, goes away, and immediately forgets what kind of man he was" (James 1:23–24).

This also ties back to my previous point concerning fatherhood. It's not enough to read that children need godly men as role models in their lives and to think to yourself, *Wow, that's a horrible situation.* You need to take that admonition personally, to ask yourself, "What kind of role model am I being for *my* children? For my wife? For my co-workers and friends?"

Remember that you'll be remembered, and ask yourself, "What will I be remembered *for*?" And if you determine that you want to be remembered as a man of God, then you also need to be prepared to take up your cross as you follow Jesus.

TAKE UP YOUR CROSS

Jesus told His followers, "If anyone desires to come after Me, let him deny himself, and take up his cross daily, and follow Me" (Luke 9:23).

There are three elements in this command: deny yourself, take up your cross every day, and follow Him. Following Jesus is the habit of obeying His Word, which we've already considered, but we sometimes forget the other two elements.

The notion of denying oneself goes against everything our culture teaches. It can feel like being a salmon, struggling against a powerful current to swim upstream for the purpose of reproducing. Yet, if the salmon does not fight that current, he will never produce another generation of salmon. And if we don't fight to deny ourselves, we also will not produce a generation of godly Christians. We won't leave a godly legacy.

It sounds almost strange to suggest that we must fight to deny ourselves. Our sinful instincts tell us just the opposite—that we need to fight tooth and nail to protect ourselves and serve ourselves. Our culture tells us constantly that we need to learn how to love ourselves. But Jesus taught that we need to learn to love others *as* we love ourselves, implying that we already know how to love ourselves. Paul told the Philippians, "Let nothing be done through selfish ambition or conceit, but in lowliness of mind let each esteem others *better than* himself" (Phil. 2:3, emphasis added).

And what does it mean to "take up your cross"? This takes us back once again to my friend Ted, who was called upon to suffer a debilitating illness that led to an early death. He could have become bitter and angry at the injustices he faced. His wife abandoned him; he suffered constant pain; he had been short-changed in life, cut down in his prime, despite having been faithful to God's Word throughout his adult life. But that is not how Ted responded; rather, he accepted his illness as something given to him by the hand of God, and he sought to imitate Christ in his suffering.

If you begin making it a habit to deny yourself, you will find that it brings a degree of suffering in its own right. It's hard work, as I've already said! But Jesus calls us to do this, to be willing to voluntarily carry our own cross, just as He did on His way to Calvary. And notice that He commands us to do this, not just once in a lifetime or even once in a while, but *daily*!

As we learn to deny ourselves and take up our cross on a daily basis, we will begin to build a legacy that lasts forever.

PERSONAL ACTIVITIES

Write an imaginary, one-sentence epitaph that you'd like to have written on your gravestone. What do you want to be remembered for? What legacy do you want to leave behind? What are you doing today to make that a reality?

MENTORING ACTIVITIES

Do a study together on the life of Stephen from Acts 6–7. What qualities did Stephen possess? Which of those qualities do you see in your mentoring partner? How can you help each other to "live according to the Spirit" rather than "according to the flesh" (Rom. 8:5)?

"We make a living by what we get, we make a life by what we give."

—Winston Churchill [1]

HOW DO I MEASURE SUCCESS?

People who compete in marathons or unique physical challenges are a special breed. I've had the privilege of serving as the medical tent chaplain for several Ironman competitions. As you get to know the competitors, you realize that very few people in the world have the skills, abilities, and perseverance to tackle the rigors associated with the physical and mental testing that occur with being an elite athlete.

In 1926, a very special elite athlete named Miss Gertrude "Trudy" Ederle completed the twenty-one-mile swim across the English Channel. At twenty years of age, she became the youngest person to accomplish this difficult task. Swimming the English Channel is no ordinary feat for even the most conditioned swimmer. In 1926, the physical conditioning, equipment, and food supplements were not anything like today's training regimen. The bitterly cold water, strong currents, stinging jellyfish, occasional shark, and waves sometimes exceeding twenty feet high make the English Channel one of the harshest swimming environments in the world.

In 1926, only five people had accomplished the feat, all of them men. For a woman even to consider this quest was beyond common sense. To make matters worse, Trudy had attempted the swim a year earlier, only to be pulled from the water by her coach when she was just six miles from victory.

The combination of many doubting spectators, withdrawal of a key sponsor, and the idea that she would change her stroke from the popular breaststroke to the new Australian crawl made the second attempt all that more challenging. But despite the challenges, Trudy Ederle climbed into the water in the early morning on August 6, 1926, and fourteen hours and thirty-one minutes later broke the record previously held by the fastest male swimmer by nearly two hours!

EIGHT ELEMENTS OF SUCCESS

My good friend Dr. Chuck Stecker, in his great work *Men of Honor, Women of Virtue*, suggested four ideas why Trudy's second attempt was successful, and I'll supplement those four with another four reasons.

1. The Plan: Her first attempt was based on the plans of others. Her second attempt was her plan, based on her unique abilities. As we'll see in a later chapter, God deliberately shapes each of His children to fit into a unique plan, to carry out some unique tasks that utilize the very character traits He has been building into us over the course of our lives. Trudy made the most of the strengths and skills that were uniquely hers.

2. The Coach: Trudy's first coach had attempted the swim himself twenty times without success. Her coach for the second attempt was Thomas Burgess, one of the five men who had successfully swum the channel. When we choose a coach to mentor us, it only makes sense to select someone who has personally experienced the things we need to learn. In this sense, Trudy selected a coach who "practiced what he preached."

3. The Encouragers: Trudy knew she would need encouragers if she was to overcome the memory of her failed first attempt. Near her was a small tugboat containing her coach, her father, her sister, and several good friends, all cheering her on. Farther back was a boat containing the press. This is a critical element of mentoring relationships, as we all need encouragement as we grow in Christlikeness. Otherwise, we can become discouraged by past failures and give up trying in the future.

4. The Decision: On her first attempt, Trudy's coach thought she had swallowed too much salt water and felt she could not continue. The moment he touched her to pull her out of the water, she was disqualified and the swim was over. On the second attempt, Trudy and her new coach had an understanding that no one could touch her or pull her out unless she agreed.[2] A good mentor will be an encourager, as I've already said, but he will also be a cheerleader, urging his mentoring partner to work through the difficulties of life without giving up. The mentor's role is to "stir up" good works and righteousness in others (Heb. 10:24).

5. The Prayer: There were many who prayed for Trudy's success. A good mentor does more than just spend time with his partner; he also spends time praying for him. Without prayer support, all our labors are in vain.

6. The Perseverance: Trudy's first attempt to swim the channel was cut short because she allowed the coach to pull her out, and she did not have a plan to cope with being sick as she was. Another fact was that her coach, who had failed this swim, really wasn't convinced she could make it. One of the most important traits of a person committed to a vision or dream is to persevere even when the world around you seems to doubt that you can accomplish what God has set upon your heart. Furthermore, just because God has given you a task to do does not mean that you won't have opposition! Perseverance will be required by anyone who sets out to run the race for Christ.

7. The Defeat of Your Foes: Trudy's foes took the form of the physical barrier of the turbulent sea, the scoffers and pundits who were not supportive, the mental challenges that stormed her mind and at times caused self-doubt, and the financial barriers that were roadblocks to attain the support necessary to attempt this challenge. Our foe is more powerful than all these forces combined—yet he has already been defeated! The devil will attempt to hinder your obedience at every turn, and you will need to remember that he has already been defeated by the same Lord who has called you to your task.

8. Leaving a Behind Good Name: Ultimately, Trudy wanted to finish what she had started. She wanted to build a lasting legacy that would encourage others in their quest to succeed. That is our goal as well: to build a lasting legacy through a lifetime of obedience to God's Word; to finish well and finish strong.

HOW DO WE MEASURE SUCCESS?

How do we go about measuring success? In one sense, it is different for every person. As God allows us to explore our gifts, talents, and diversity, we are able to seek His plan for our lives. From the world's standpoint, success is often measured by fame, beauty, fortune, position, power, prominence, education, achievements, and records. The legacy of a job well done is seen through the eyes of a person's peers, the media, or the pride our supporters have in what we have done. For Trudy Ederle, being successful in life took the form of swimming across the English Channel. Until she died in 2003, Trudy was a legend and sought after by those who could grow close to her.

What is success for the Christian? How might it be measured differently? The aforementioned measurements of worldly successes have their place in a Christian's life, but a greater measurement of success comes from knowing we are in God's will and plan—and in this sense, the measurement of success is the same for every Christian. The question that immediately comes to mind is this: Are we using our God-given gifts, talents, and wisdom to live a glorified life that beckons others to follow Christ?

When we look at a definition of biblical success, it is important to think about what is being glorified or to whom the credit is given. The world would tell us that success is about *being* important rather than *doing* what's important. Our unsaved peers would say it's about those measurable things like a bank account, the size of our office, our possessions, and so forth.

But the Bible testifies to an audience of one—the One, God Almighty. He is the one who will judge and measure our lives. And best of all, it matters not what success we have in the sports arena, workplace, playground, or board room. Our financial balance sheet won't matter, nor will whatever possessions we have in our homes or storage lockers. And those good deeds we did won't get us into heaven because it's not about works.

What will matter is a personal relationship with the living God. He is the one who matters. And a relationship with God isn't about accumulation, but just the reverse; it's about sacrifice. The worldly possessions we strive to protect, keep, and multiply are but filthy rags to the King of kings. He wants us to be "givers," not "takers." He wants a servant's heart. Our position with God isn't about how well we are dressed, what foods we eat, or what titles are in front of our name, but about one important thing: faithfulness.

What can we learn from Trudy Ederle's swim? I believe there are eight guidelines we can follow that will help us define a successful life:

1. The Plan. Maintain holy living. There is no greater obstacle to becoming successful than sin. It can pop up in the middle of great accomplishments, thereby stealing the joy and legacy that would otherwise define the events. By allowing the Holy Spirit to work within our lives, we can find the guidance that will direct our paths and keep us from falling into sin.

Another facet of the plan is to maintain godly relationships with other believers. God will use the power of relationships to keep us from falling into the grip of sin. First we need to have a growing relationship with our heavenly Father through prayer, meditation, and Bible study. And then there is Christian fellowship, the body of believers, who surround us with their love and accountability. It is the obedient Christian who can claim the victory at the end of the race.

The power of relationships is so important to building success. For example, there is an interesting paradox in the business world. The skills, training, abilities, credentials, and qualifications that got you your job rarely help you keep it. It comes down to your ability to adapt, learn new approaches, and make connections to others, as well as how you can build a viable relationship to senior management. In the same way, building godly relationships will help us stay on track with God's plan for our lives.

2. The Coach. Thomas Burgess was to Trudy what a spiritual mentor is to us. We all need a coach, mentor, true friend who can help guide us and direct our paths. We need people who have invested in us and can paint a powerful blessing and vision before us so we will not fail. Authentic spiritual mentoring is about developing a caring concern and a genuine love for others, modeling Christlike attitudes and behavior. The coach encourages his partner to get beyond past failures, while also spurring him on to become more and more like Christ.

3. The Encouragers. Trudy surrounded herself with people who would urge her on through encouragement, while she kept the journalists (who had not been encouraging) at a safe distance in a separate boat. If you surround yourself with people who cannot look beyond their own negative feelings and the negativity of the world around us, you have the wrong people in your life. Yes, even well-meaning church friends can stifle your creativity and vision with a forecast that will cloud your thinking. Find people who can speak positively into your life and future. Like Trudy, put those inspirational people in close proximity who can chant the songs of praise and blessing. This does not mean that we disregard wise counsel, of course, but it does mean that we refuse to allow past failures or our own shortcomings to prevent us from pushing on toward the goal of finishing well and strong.

4. The Decision. God gives you the vision or dream for how to approach life. If you have validated the idea through prayer, Bible study, and wise counsel, then move forward, looking for the open doors that only God can provide. Know the purpose that God has put into your heart. The apostle Paul finished the race because he knew what his race entailed. Jesus finished the work the Father gave Him because He focused on God's plan. Both knew their reasons for being here and stayed true to their work. Stay true to the purpose that God has given you.

5. The Prayer. Behind any successful Christian person is a legion of people praying for his protection, health, vision, and direction. To be successful, we need to pray and have others praying for us. Prayer, at its root, is discovering the heart of God so we can live the obedient life. Prayer is a commandment of God; He has directed us to pray to Him, and to Him alone. During times of suffering, we must turn to God for help; in times of comfort, we must express our gratitude to God; and when all goes well with us, we must still praise Him daily for who He is, asking that He continue to show us His mercy and grant us our daily needs. The psalmist reminds us of the power of prayer: "Deliver me out of the mire, and let me not sink; let me be delivered from those who hate me, and out of the deep waters" (Ps. 69:14).

6. The Perseverance. Whether leading or prodding others, tackling life's problems, or contributing to some great cause, perseverance is crucial to success. "Hang in there, baby!" is more than an expression of encouragement; it is good advice for a disciple. Perseverance is an essential ingredient in our quest to be successful. On his second tour through Galilee with His disciples, Christ shared the parable of the sower (Luke 8:5–15) as His encouragement for them to persevere. "But the seed on good soil stands for those with a noble and good heart, who hear the word, retain it, and *by persevering* produce a crop" (Luke 8:15 NIV, emphasis added). Notice that important phrase: "by persevering." We can only produce a good crop if we persevere, and this also suggests that we will encounter opposition when we strive to do God's will. Our determination to "stick to it" has a lot to do with getting the right results—God's results.

7. The Defeat of Your Foes. Life in this world is filled with sorrow and disappointment. It can be very easy for a Christian to become discouraged, to think that the future is bleak and hopeless—but we must not give in to that sort of thinking. We are like people living inside a besieged city during a time of war. The enemy surrounds us on all sides and won't allow any food or supplies to get through. But we know that, afar off, our Leader has already defeated the enemy, destroying his armies and breaking his power utterly. It is only a matter of time until that victory is completed, when our Leader will come and drive away the besieging forces, setting us free from our suffering and hardship. We just need to be faithful to what He wants us doing until He gets here. Remember this always: the foe is already defeated![3]

8. Leaving Behind a Good Name. Proverbs 10:7 says, "The memory of the righteous is blessed, but the name of the wicked will rot." What kind of legacy are you leaving? Would family members beyond two generations be impacted by your life? Being successful cannot come at the sacrifice of our good name. As a young dad, I continually reminded our boys that they carried the Grassi name. Today I chatted with my grandson and reminded him that his father passed along a name and legacy that needs protecting. If you don't have children, then you can leave a good name among those who knew you best, whether friends or work associates or people who crossed your path.

A poem from an unknown author emerged in 1949. It helps us understand why striving to be a successful Christian is important to building a good legacy.

Excellence can be obtained if you:
. . . care more than others think is wise;
. . . risk more than others think is safe;
. . . dream more than others think is practical;
. . . expect more than others think is possible.[4]

PERSONAL ACTIVITIES

Put together a list of commitments in your life, a list of those things that are not negotiable. These are your top priorities, the things you will do or protect even if it means that other, less important things don't get done. For example, you might put "personal devotions" on the list, meaning that you are committed to spending time alone in Bible study and prayer each day. Be sure to keep it practical, listing things that can be measured on a daily or weekly basis. Writing "become a man of God" is rather vague and hard to measure, while personal devotions can be done each day and can be shared with an accountability partner.

The object is not to have a list to beat yourself up with or another "to do" list, but to simply have a general guide and framework on which you can base your decisions and commitments. When asked to volunteer for something, or when you consider a life-change (job, education, etc.), it is helpful to see how it fits into your overall plan that you thought about within the context of Scripture, your wife's input, the power of the Holy Spirit, and so forth.

MENTORING ACTIVITIES

Both partners should make a personal list of commitments (see above). Share your lists together, helping each other to refine them and to include things that might have been overlooked. In the coming month, hold each other accountable for your lists. "How did you do on your personal devotions last week?" "Did you attend your son's soccer game yesterday, as a way of attaining your commitment to spend time with family?"

*"Success is not final, failure is not fatal:
it is the courage to continue that counts."*

—Winston Churchill[1]

SUCCESS, SIGNIFICANCE, OR BOTH?

Our good friends Bill and Betty are living models of people who have worldly success with a focus upon eternal significance. Bill started out as an apprentice plumber with the idea that his hard work would someday pay for the mounting bills associated with being newly married. Within a short period of time, his commitment paid off as he became a journeyman plumber. His work ethic and drive propelled him into a robust career.

Bill was a guy who really didn't enjoy working for others, as his core values often conflicted with the rough-and-tumble atmosphere associated with the union bosses. Bill finally decided to go out on his own and develop a plumbing supply house business that provided a variety of products to plumbers all over his region. His business became very successful as people appreciated his honest approach to customer care.

But during this time of business growth and expansion, a terrible tragedy struck their home. Their son Jeff had recently turned sixteen and had just gotten his driver's license. He took Bill's car out one evening to go to the movies, taking delight in his new-found sense of independence—and he never returned home alive. On his way back from the theater, Jeff was struck head-on by a drunk driver and was killed instantly. The shock of this event traumatized the family, but they were intentional about making a decision not to be bitter but to become stronger and more united and to utilize the tragedy as a stepping-stone to model their faith in God's plan for their lives.

Many couples might have begun to question their faith at this point, asking, "How could a good God have let this happen?" But Bill and Betty never doubted that God is faithful and just and that He had permitted this deep sorrow to touch their lives for some greater purpose. They had no idea what God's purpose might have been, but they clung firmly to the conviction that He was in control and could be trusted.

As they began to heal over the following years, the couple rediscovered that building a business required a lot of hard work and dedication, yet the primary importance in their lives continued to be following God's Word. They were active members of their church and regularly got involved with Bible studies. They took to heart the many lessons learned about work, finances, and loving others. Some of those lessons were difficult to learn, like having patience with people, listening more and talking less, and choosing to commit to the priorities. They took time to develop those qualities, but they knew all along that God was helping them to grow into the image of Christ (Eph. 4:13–15).

As Bill's reputation grew, so did the profit line of his company. Soon additional stores were opened in surrounding communities. He became known in the communities for his humble heart and generous spirit. His business grew and allowed him the opportunity to purchase a beautiful home for his family of five. He was able to afford a nice ski boat that was docked at his cabin on the lake, and a couple of newer vehicles.

Most important to Bill and Betty's success was what they were able to contribute back to their community. They shared their wealth with the needy and downtrodden. As major contributors to a battered women's shelter and the local Gospel Mission Home, they saw their donations create lifelines for many people. His Rotary Club even voted him the president and regional representative for their chapter.

Bill and Betty decided to partner with some other Christian business leaders to support a church building program that provided the building materials for pastors desiring to develop small churches. Working with architects and other builders, they packaged the twelve-hundred-square-foot sanctuary so that it could be dropped off at a location and then erected by members of the new church. The only thing a pastor had to provide was a deed to the property, a crew to erect the building, and the promise to properly maintain the facility.

Over one hundred small churches got their start from the generosity of Bill and Betty and their friends. To this family, being successful was not measured by their personal wealth and prosperous business, but by using their resources to do "God-sized" projects that have eternal significance.

FINDING A BALANCE

In his masterful work *Success to Significance*, Lloyd Reeb wrote:

> Society is undergoing a fundamental shift from "material want" to "meaning want," with ever larger numbers of people reasonably secure in terms of living standards, but feeling they lack significance in their lives. A transition from "material want" to "meaning want" is not a prediction that men and women will cease being materialistic; no social indicator points to such a possibility. It is a prediction that ever more millions will expect both pleasant living standards and a broad sense that their lives possess purpose. This is a conundrum, as meaning is much more difficult to acquire than material possessions."[2]

Bill and Betty found that balance and they were able to start well and finish well. They recognized that being successful had to include doing things of significance. Their faith was strong and, along with using gifts and resources, they determined to make this world a better place. Their desire was to be good stewards of God's money. They discovered the truth that the prophet Micah explained for us when he wrote, "He has shown you, O man, what is good; and what does the LORD require of you but to do justly, to love mercy, and to walk humbly with your God?" (Mic. 6:8). They also embraced God's promise in Malachi 3:10: "'Bring all the tithes into the storehouse, that there may be food in My house, and try Me now in this,' says the LORD of hosts, 'if I will not open for you the windows of heaven and pour out for you such blessing that there will not be room enough to receive it.'"

Micah's words can lead to costly obedience. Implementing the prophet's words requires self-sacrifice, a heart to serve others, and a

Christlike vision. Much in our culture directs people to "get and take all you can." We are a "feel good, got to have it now" society. There is not much in our media that projects the value of having a generous spirit or putting others above self. It is more about the greed and selfishness that creates a horrendous appetite for having more, bigger, better, and the best.

Malachi also helps us understand how to be faithful to God even when things go well. That's right—not just when things go wrong, but also when they go right. It's just as dangerous to a man's soul to gain wealth and success as to suffer failure and poverty—maybe even more so. But my friends Bill and Betty took God's words to heart and learned to be very generous in their tithing and support of things with eternal significance. The more they earned, the larger a percentage of those earnings went to the Lord's work. It's easy to increase our standards of living as our income increases, which leads to the sense that somehow we never make enough money. But Bill and Betty avoided that trap by maintaining the same modest expectations in their lives, even when they could have spent more. They simply gave a larger and larger percentage of their income to God.

Years ago, there wasn't much thought about retirement, building a legacy, or passing on any substantial material wealth to the next generation. The parents of the first half of the twentieth century had all they could handle by just trying to provide for the immediate needs of their families. In the mid-1900s, people's basic needs—food, shelter, and transportation—were being met. Many seniors who weren't connected with faith were asking the question, "Is this all there is to life?" For many, their jobs were their life.

Many in our current retirement generation believed that fulfillment might come by purchasing a motor home and touring the country, or acquiring a mountain cabin where they could hunt and fish, or moving to a warm climate where they could spend their idle time playing golf or swimming. But at the end of their careers, too many of these individuals felt abandoned, alone, and fearful.

Our goal needs to be somewhere in between these two extremes. We certainly want to provide the basic necessities for ourselves and our families, and we do need to develop a good work ethic. It is not a good testimony to the world around us if we slack off in our jobs or don't pay our bills. Being successful in a career is not equivalent to being unsuccessful in our Christian lives. But at the same time, we must be constantly on guard against the trap of materialism. It's very easy to increase our expectations and standard of living when our finances increase, but God has promised to bless those who give generously of their bounty. Always remember that everything you earn is a gift from God, not something that the world (or God) owes you.

Someone once asked me if he was being unfaithful because he had many possessions that some people envied. He felt guilty and confused as to what to do with his wealth and prosperity. I encouraged him that God seems to bless a few with great prosperity because only a few people like my friend know how to live within their prosperity while being a giving person.

Again Lloyd Reeb offers some ideas: "Each day, between ten and twelve thousand people in the United States turn fifty. One in four Americans are over fifty, and the fifty to sixty-four year old age group is expected to grow by 50 percent by 2015, making the mature consumer market one that demands attention. But how many of those people focus on their longing for significance?"[3]

SHIFTING OUR FOCUS

What can cause a shift in our hearts and focus from a life of success to a life of significance? For some, it's the long haul of grinding the gears of frustration and failure over a life lived out. Typically, once people get to retirement age, they begin to start processing life a little differently. For others, there will be a quick shift when the transition of life has a trigger event, such as the loss of a relative, the children leaving the nest, a divorce, a major business failure, a major physical illness, or a child who has gone wild. For me, it was a combination of the life-threatening surgery that I faced when I was thirty-seven years of age (which I describe in the Introduction) and the frustrations I was feeling about the turmoil and stress in my life as I endeavored to *be* important instead of focusing upon *doing* what was important. The non-malignant brain tumor is very uncommon, especially at the age it showed up in me. The event was one of those times when a person evaluates his life, its meaning, God's purpose, and the importance of having both short-term and long-term goals. As the firstborn male on either side of my ancestry, I felt a great deal of stress to succeed by the standards of my generation. No one had been to college, most of my family had menial jobs, and wealth was something we only heard about.

In my search for success, I spent too much time focusing on too many things (being a good Christian husband, outstanding father, administrator, bass tournament competitor, great hunter, author, Bible study leader, board member, and so forth). In retrospect, trying to be successful in many areas all at the same time was an unrealistic goal. There was little thought about how to organize my life in terms of a life plan that had direction toward things of eternal significance.

It matters not how you begin the process of transforming to a life focused upon significance; it's just important that you begin. What is it that you have placed on your top priority list that testifies to your commitment to building a life that is significant? Ideally, of course, we understand this distinction when we're young, as Daniel did, but it is never too late to redirect our priorities and shift our focus. God is faithful to give us opportunities to serve Him with excellence throughout our lives, and we need to be quick to see those opportunities and to pounce on them. It is easy to become content with things the way they are, not wanting to rock the boat or being afraid to risk failure, but that leads us only to being in the rut of the ordinary. We need to get out of the ordinary and pounce upon the extraordinary!

When a young man is first starting out in his career, he is willing to tackle things that may seem difficult, even foreign, to his natural talent, but he will take the risk because of the rewards that he can foresee coming from it—often financial rewards. But as we get older, we tend to concentrate more on being efficient, effective, and employable, rather than on taking risks or pursuing our greatest passions. As we get older in our walk with God, we need to frequently rekindle those passions and renew our focus on pursuing excellence for the kingdom of God. We need to remind ourselves that we are more concerned with significance in God's eyes than we are with success in the world's eyes.

This shift in focus comes from within. The movement to significance is about changing the way we view life and the God-given opportunities before us. One of the key things that needs to be determined is how God has made you. As much as I would like to be an astronaut, it would not be appropriate for me to set this as a goal. I don't like heights, computers frustrate me, and I don't function well when I'm in confined places for long periods of time. In space, there is nothing to hunt or catch and no wildlife to capture on my camera. In short, God did not create me with those passions, my academic background doesn't match the requirements, and there is no one in my cultural heritage who is linked with space exploration.

There is definitely a balance between success and significance, and the goal is to strive for both simultaneously. We work to be successful in our careers, but not because it brings us wealth or security. We strive for success because we are working for the King of kings, and we do not want to present mediocre work to Him. We want our work and accomplishments to be significant by God's standards, whether or not that aligns with the world's standards. As we maintain this balance on a daily basis, we are well on the way to finishing well and finishing strong.

PERSONAL ACTIVITIES

One way to quantitatively identify God's direction for your life is to put together a little grid that will help you focus on your distinctive traits. Make a list of those things that you have achieved and that are measurable accomplishments. Make a second list of *opportunities* to do things of significance. What is on the horizon of possibilities that could change your life and the lives of those around you? What are the things that you do well? What are the things that give you the greatest joy? Along with your feelings, be intentional about your self-assessment.

While thinking about the concepts described on your lists, set those aside and create a separate matrix of personal experiences. On the Y-axis, write out the things you've experienced that involved some of your accomplishments, or tasks that came easily to you. On the

X-axis, rate those experiences on a scale of 1 to 5, with 5 being the highest. What brought you the greatest delight and felt relatively easy or natural?

Accomplishments	1	2	3	4	5

Begin praying about what God would have you do. Ask mentors in your life what they see in you as your talents and gifts. What doors of opportunity is God opening that you might step through? Are you daily in God's Word, asking Him to reveal to you what your future foundation could look like?

As we enter into the life of significance, we need to recognize that quantity is not a good substitute for quality. Finishing strong is not about trying to put twenty pounds of adventure into a ten-pound bag. It is about finding the best of the best. Cut out those things that don't bring you joy and begin to be directed to the goals that God has placed upon your heart.

MENTORING ACTIVITIES

Both partners should construct a grid of personal experiences described above. There are ways to quantify the goals or adventures that come before you. As you consider the possibilities, evaluate them using the matrix.

With your mentor, discuss your core values from the heart, spirit, impact to others, personal joy, and personal growth that could bring about joy to yourself and others.

Work together to analyze each person's strengths and weaknesses. What are the kinds of things that jump out to you? What is it telling you about your point of focus? What sorts of ministries might be a natural fit for each of you?

One thing to consider when filling out your chart is the limitations that might pose a problem. For instance, if you don't like traveling, then considering an around-the-world trip to help spread the gospel is probably not a good idea. While being adventurous, it may produce too much stress. If you are afraid of spiders and snakes, then doing a roughing-it trip to the back woods of Africa may not be your cup of tea. As you ponder your move from success to significance, don't devalue your hidden aspirations or fears. As we get older, those things seem to magnify themselves in the activities we pursue.

Experiment and try different things. It is rare that the first time out of your shell of comfort you will find that your first idea was the right pursuit for the rest of your life. Oftentimes, only after trying a variety of things do you finally discover the perfect fit for your personal profile. This will lead to a God-given joy you will find as you finish strong.

"Nothing can stop the man with the right mental attitude from achieving his goal; nothing on earth can help a man with the wrong mental attitude."

—**Thomas Jefferson**[1]

WHAT DOES A MAN OF SIGNIFICANCE LOOK LIKE?

In the course of life, I've had the privilege to meet many prominent and successful men. I have crossed paths with NFL coaches and MVPs, major political leaders from various countries, Hollywood movie stars, famous business leaders and consultants, best-selling authors, outdoor sports television personalities, and many well-known Christian leaders.

While I appreciate the many contributions and achievements of all these men and women, what impresses me the most are the precious few who intimately know God, have an earnest desire to make Him known, and seek to make eternal contributions that give God the honor and glory. And by the way, I certainly don't consider my encounters with the successful men to in any way suggest that by association I must therefore be significant. Significance comes by each person taking on the vision and daily work of trying to live a life that glorifies our Lord.

Many of the people on my short list of *most significant models* have already gone home to be with the Lord. Some are waiting for God's home-calling, as their age and health have placed their mark on their lives and strength and they are no longer able to provide the amount of ministry they did in the past. And there are a few young people who make my list of "significant" people who are contributing greatly to build God's kingdom. Without being totally biased, I would say our twin sons, Dan and Tom, would be among those precious souls who are endeavoring to start well and have a vision to finish strong.

I'm sure your list might be different from mine and your qualifications for the list will also differ. I look at a person's qualifications to be on my list through the lens of Scripture—sort of a Proverbs 31 for both men and women. But let me tell you first about a guy who exemplifies the scriptural attributes you will find later in this chapter.

Jack Countryman is a friend of mine who was fortunate to be raised in a Christian home with great parents who loved the Lord and modeled what it meant to walk daily with Christ. As a young person, he was drawn to the challenge and rewards that naturally come with competing in sports. He played football and golf, ran track, and generally absorbed the benefits that come from having good coaches and mentors in his life. He was never content sitting on the bench, and worked hard to be involved in the game. He was and is a participant! His passion for excellence drove him to excel in sports. He recalls praying, "Lord, do not put me on the bench." He said to me in our interview, "When you're in the game, you are doing something—you're engaged—you have something to focus on."[2]

After graduating from a major college where he was a football star, Jack became involved in developing and managing fitness centers and health spas. His passion and focus, along with the faithful efforts of his wife, allowed him to establish a chain of thirty-six facilities around the country. In his mid forties, he employed more than five hundred people and was at the top of the heap when it came to deploying good management practices. By all worldly standards, he was a successful and significant person in his field. He wasn't born successful, but he discovered ways to succeed. He worked diligently for his outcomes.

As he pondered the future, God kept speaking to him about the clients attending his many studios. He recognized that the most joyful people and the ones who seem to deal with the many issues that life throws at them were strong believers in Christ and His Word. They were men and women who had great faith in Christ Jesus. Here's how Jack described the things that God taught him:

While we helped clients to eat nutritiously, lose weight, gain strength, build muscles, and increase flexibility that primarily helped the physical part of their lives, we found that, for people to be really healthy, they had to address the emotional and spiritual parts of their lives. It was especially significant when the spiritual element was addressed.

When I spoke with clients and they were receptive to spiritual matters, their progress in transforming their body, mind, and spirit helped propel these people in their stated goals.

For me, my personal transformation had to begin at home. When I looked at our sons Bret and Jason, I realized how important it would be to model a Spirit-filled life.

My business was going through some challenges with the economy. God was drawing me into His Word and opportunities to share the things I was learning about living a joy-filled life. Then one day, my wife and I sat down at the kitchen table and decided to start a Christian publishing company. We compiled our first book and sold it out of the trunk of our car wherever we went.

We knew nothing about Christian publishing and neither my wife nor I were journalism majors. We just let the Holy Spirit work through us as we wrote our books. God took our love for people and our combined marketing and selling abilities to develop ideas that seemed to inspire people.

FIVE PRINCIPLES OF SUCCESSFUL MINISTRY

Jack and his wife built their company on a few important principles:

1. No matter how much success you experience, you have to remain open to ideas. In fact, I'll go beyond this and suggest that the more success you experience, the more you need to remain open to new ideas. God uses our skills and experiences and unique traits to fit us for a unique ministry in His service, and that can lead to the temptation to think that we're experts. We're not; He is. And He uses the input of other people to help us shape and refine the work He's given us to do.

2. Stay in the game. As I approach the age of retirement by the world's standards, I am committed not to retire, but to "refire," to be always rekindling my determination to run the race all the way to the finish line. But there is a strong temptation throughout one's life to give up, to throw in the towel, to say "I just can't do this" and go sit on the bench. In order to finish well, we must first finish—and in order to finish, we need to stay in the game, to never stop fighting against the evil one and our own fleshly desires.

3. Be teachable. I always come back to the principle that a man who finishes well is a man who remains teachable all his life. As we go through this book, you will see that there is no time in life when a man is impervious to temptation or exempt from failure; nobody ever fully becomes like Christ this side of eternity. We need to remain open to the leading of the Holy Spirit throughout our lives, and He uses the input of others as well as circumstances beyond our control to teach us.

4. Go with what God wants you to do. Life is filled with challenges and opportunities and distractions—more of them than we could pursue even if we didn't have other priorities waiting for us. Find the ministry and calling that God has for you, and stay focused on it. We'll help you in the process of determining what that calling is throughout this book; your job is to *do it.*

5. Look for and accept the challenges that God gives you. This goes along with what I said above, but it expands on it a bit. It's true that there are more needs in the world than one man can meet, but it's also true that our own fleshly inclinations can persuade us to simply be lazy and not worry about meeting any of those needs. You can't meet every need, but look for them anyway. When we have that attitude, God will bring us exciting ministry opportunities, and His Holy Spirit will help us weed out the ones to which we're not suited.

SERVING IN A RICHER WAY

Jack Countryman explained to me, "The Lord inspires us to daily learn more about His Word. God promises us wisdom when we are obedient to His Word. Meet people's needs, and He will bless you in ways you didn't expect."

On December 12, 1994, when Jack was sixty-five, the age most people think about retirement, Thomas Nelson Publishers offered to buy out his company if he and his wife, Marsha, would continue their work of creating books that encourage others. They accepted the invitation, and today in his eighties, Jack Countryman has been involved in creating more than eight hundred titles that have sold over eighty-six million copies. He no longer works fourteen-hour days like he did when he was in the health studio business. His passion is to see people become strong in the body, mind, and spirit. His life is balanced with his work, family, and time for recreation. He still shoots in the seventies in golf and has energy that will outlast the most avid outdoorsmen.

Jack has told me, "The most fruitful years come after you are sixty-five years of age. By then, you have made a host of mistakes and hopefully learned from them and you know more than you have ever known before. If you remain teachable, God will allow you to serve in a richer way. After all, you spent all those years learning and throughout your life you must apply those lessons. It is our responsibility as disciples to stay fruitful as long as we can until we are taken home."

A CLEAR VISION

One of the many things I've learned from Jack's life and from watching other significant people who prosper is that you must have a vision and focus for the future. The best time for a person to consider how he can be significant and have an impact for the Lord is when he is young. True joy, peace, and comfort happen because a person is intentional about setting the right course for his thinking. Scripture tells us that our first priority should be to consider those things that have eternal value.

Seeking the pity of others because we are trying to do things like fasting or tithing only demonstrates our dependence on people rather than God for ultimate approval. We should do these things because God will direct and bless us. Pursuing wealth to the detriment of our faith reveals that we draw more security from our possessions than from the Father who gives us all things to enjoy.

Rather than trying to figure out how you will take from the world, consider what you can give to others. Instead of finding immediate gratification, look for opportunities to invest part of your life into things that have an eternal dimension and eternal value. God isn't asking everyone to become a Mother Teresa. I believe He wants us to take our gifts, talents, contacts, and love for Jesus to influence one person at a time, right where He has planted us.

You measure life in heartbeats and breaths of creative moments and times to share your life with others. Ultimately, it is about relationships—relationship with God, then family, and with those in our sphere of influence. I believe that God wants us to enjoy and utilize our influence for His glory. Experiences, especially those things where we vividly experience the hand of God, are places we must learn from, and then teach those lessons to others.

The psalmist wrote, "Search me, O God, and know my heart; try me, and know my anxieties; and see if there is any wicked way in me, and lead me in the way everlasting" (Ps. 139:23–24). We tend to read those verses and reflect upon our outward actions, which is certainly a legitimate response—but we forget to examine our private thoughts as well. Paul expanded on this theme of God's searching our hearts to include our minds:

> I beseech you therefore, brethren, by the mercies of God, that you present your bodies a living sacrifice, holy, acceptable to God, which is your reasonable service. And do not be conformed to this world, but be transformed by the renewing of your mind, that you may prove what is that good and acceptable and perfect will of God. (Rom. 12:1–2)

Just as we become what we put in our bodies, so we also become what we put in our minds. We can guide our thoughts by what we place in our minds and hearts. Paul went on to say in Romans 12:3, "For I say, through the grace given to me, to everyone who is among you, not to think of himself more highly than he ought to think, but to think soberly, as God has dealt to each one a measure of faith." One of the important elements of thinking correctly is to consider that other people are better than you! This is the opposite of what the world teaches, but it is at the center of being like Christ.

REASSESSING OUR PRIORITIES

As we contemplate what makes our lives significant, let's think about some questions that we should ask ourselves. And we need to ask these questions frequently, because we can drift off course without being aware of it otherwise.

* *How much is enough?* Enough money, enough possessions, enough friends, enough popularity, enough power, or enough fame. Is "enough" ever really enough? We will discuss this further in a later chapter, but the basic answer to this question is this: there is *never* enough! Change this question to: "How much godliness is enough? How much of Christ's character in me is enough?" That is the better goal.

* *How do I feel about my career? Is there a pathway to another job that allows me to move more directly to my life goal?* This, of course, raises the question, "What *is* my life goal?" We will discuss this in detail in another chapter, but for now we'll summarize by saying that our goal is to finish well and strong. If your present job is eating up all your time and energy, it might be hindering you in that goal.

* *Am I living a balanced life (faith, work, family, leisure, private time, chores, hobbies, friendships)?* This is the corollary to the previous question. Just as we don't want a career that hinders us from finishing well, so we also don't want to allow our lives to become unbalanced in other directions. There are many forces that can claim our allegiance at the expense of our walk with God—hobbies, chores, consuming friendships, even work at your local church. We need to frequently reassess how we're spending our time and energies to ensure that we are running the race to the utmost.

* *What inspires me the most? How can I make time for more of that?* When I'm at my best, when my energies seem never-ending, and when I'm in my sweet spot for the gifts, skills, and abilities God has given me, I enjoy sharing the Word of God, teaching others lessons of life I've learned, and helping people understand how not to make the mistakes I have.

* *Who are the people I most admire?* We learn best by seeing something in action. If you want to learn to play golf, you watch the pros and imitate them. Paul told his readers to imitate him (1 Cor. 4:16; 11:1) because he was striving to imitate Christ. Ultimately, of

course, we all imitate Jesus, but it can be very helpful to also have role models from your own lifetime. We started this book with some snapshots of men who finished well and strong; find some that you admire and imitate their examples.

✱ *What do I believe and why?* These are things that are nonnegotiable. We will address this topic more in depth in a later chapter, but for now you should consider what things in your life you would pour yourself into, even if other things had to be neglected. The non-negotiable priorities will reveal to you where your treasure lies. Does your treasure lie in eternity, or in the things of this world? This is a critical issue to resolve first and foremost if you want to finish well and strong.

Moving from success to significance may involve giving up the thrill of the deal to capture the joy of helping to transform a life. When you can look at challenges as opportunities to model a Christ-like life, you realize that your primary work isn't measured by worldly success, but by how God is using you for kingdom work.

When we adopt a Christ-centered perspective about life, then challenges, tension, and stress-filled situations can become stepping-stones toward a deeper relationship with Him. In Philippians 4:6–7, Paul encourages his readers to "Be anxious for nothing, but in everything by prayer and supplication, with thanksgiving, let your requests be made known to God; and the peace of God, which surpasses all understanding, will guard your hearts and minds through Christ Jesus." And Jesus told His disciples, "do not worry about your life. . . . Which of you by worrying can add one cubit to his stature?" (Matt. 6:25, 27).

When you begin to see life as God sees it, you look at people differently. Instead of looking at them as a paycheck or something to fix, you see them at a deeper level. You look for opportunities to share your faith. As you steadfastly focus on Jesus and His Word, you change from the inside out. Your attitudes change and more and more you desire to be a "giver" instead of a "getter." Your focus is "how can I help you?" as opposed to "how can this person help me?" Long-term influence and legacy become your goals instead of short-term advantage.

In other words, you become focused on laying up treasures in heaven (Matt. 6:19–21). You now see vacations as an opportunity to refresh yourself so you can build into your family great truths and special times, rather than seeing vacations as a distraction from your next appointment.

Let's say that your employer tempts you with a promotion: if you become sold out to the company and pay your dues, they'll make you a full partner! You can now evaluate that offer in light of the personal sacrifices you will have to make. The old saying comes back to remind you that "people don't care about how much you know until they know how much you care."[3]

The Bible is full of examples of men who followed through and were rewarded for keeping focused on God's plan for their lives. Caleb explored the promised land with bravery and persistence, trusting in the promise of the Lord when everyone else was too afraid to continue. Because of his dedication and willingness to stay with God's plan, God promised that his descendants would enter the promised land (Num. 14:24).

The apostle Paul made it his life's work to encourage and strengthen the church and preach the good news of Christ to the Gentiles. He persevered through beatings, imprisonment, a shipwreck that left him stranded in the open sea for a night and a day, sleep deprivation, and attacks of criticism from his own flock (2 Cor. 11:22–33). Yet he experienced an inner strength and peace that enabled him to further the gospel like no one else.

Jesus stated plainly, "My food is to do the will of Him who sent Me, and to finish His work" (John 4:34). To do God's will, Jesus endured public ridicule, long days of travel, and finally a cruel death on a cross. Because of this, "God also has highly exalted Him and given Him the name which is above every name, that at the name of Jesus every knee should bow, of those in heaven, and of those on earth, and of those under the earth" (Phil. 2:9–10).

All of these men were committed to causes that were greater than themselves; they took on missions from God and were determined to do His will above all else. And how does one discover the will of God? Many hundreds of books have been written on this subject, but one of the best places to start is Micah 6:8: "He has shown you, O man, what is good; and what does the LORD require of you but to do justly, to love mercy, and to walk humbly with your God?" From this verse alone, we can recognize that the will of God for you is to do justly, love mercy, and walk humbly with Him. The man who steadfastly does these things will have little difficulty recognizing God's will in other areas of his life.

And, of course, one of the highest callings from God is the honor of rearing children and seeing them mature in their faith (Phil. 2:19–24). For those who do not have children of their own or for those whose children are out of the nest helping with those kids who need the love of an adult is a very gratifying experience. Just as you can learn godliness by imitating other godly men, so also can children learn by imitating you!

THE GOALS OF OUR LIVES

Beginning in my grade school years, what made a successful person was being mapped out in my mind. If you wanted to be picked first for a team, you had to be the best or most popular. If you desired the teacher's approval, you needed to study hard and behave yourself. If you wanted friends, you needed to be a friend. Teachers and administrators admired and respected students who took on leadership tasks, like being on the traffic patrol or a milk monitor. (For those too young to know what a milk monitor was, the milk monitor collected a nickel from each student who wanted cold milk at lunch.) If you were a good student and succeeded in school, chances are your parents repaid you with more play time and toys.

But I quickly discovered that as you compete for something, there is always someone better than you. Maybe it was a student in another class or on another team or someone who was good at playing a musical instrument or a person who excelled in academics. For many who worked through high school and went on to college, the challenges and rewards became greater. You sought the best colleges for academics, you competed for scholarships against other students, and finally after graduation your focus became the job market. Whether a person went directly into the trades after high school or was a college graduate, another set of questions had to be addressed: What job would best fit my skills? Who would pay the most for my talents? What would make me happy? What choice of jobs offered the best chance for advancement and success?

Once in your selected career, the drive to make the most money, accumulate the most possessions, become a journeyman in your trade, have a corner office, or become a partner in the firm became a goal. And there were a few who had a vision of retiring early, and that became their dream. Many of us looked for fulfillment, happiness, and satisfaction in all these things, but too often found emptiness, loneliness, and frustration. Several people I know who have been on this track tell me that when they were in the mix to succeed, enough was never enough.

Bob Buford says in his book *Halftime* that the first half of our lives is spent learning how to make a living, and the second half has the promise of being about how to make a life. He wrote, "For me the transition into the afternoon of life was a time for reordering my time and my treasure, for reconfiguring my values and my vision of what life could be. It represented more than a renewal; it was a new beginning. It was more than a reality check; it was a fresh and leisurely look into the holiest chamber of my own heart, affording me, at last, an opportunity to respond to my soul's deepest longings."[4]

Part of the problem has to do with our focus, whether we are inward focused or outward focused. Typically for the majority of our lives, we are inward focused. We are concerned with our own happiness, with getting more material possessions, with our reputation and self-importance. But being outward focused requires a special discipline and perspective that only comes with maturity. Outward focus suggests a selfless attitude and an intentional decision to follow God's plan for your life and to seek ways to serve others. When confronted with an opportunity, you study the matter and look for consequences that best project a servant's heart and a way forward where everybody wins.

I don't mean that we compromise our faith, core values, or soul. Simply put, we find ways to see the good in others and ourselves so we can help create a peaceful environment. The Bible give us great examples of men who, despite hardships, mistakes, and disappointments, chose to consistently follow God and keep His Word.

Look at the lives of Joseph, Joshua, Caleb, Samuel, Elijah, Jeremiah, Daniel, John, Paul, and Peter as guys who finished strong. They faced their challenges, disappointments, setbacks, and distractions as eventual stepping-stones in realizing God's plan for their lives.

Jack Countryman discovered these qualities in his forties. Many people never realize the importance of these characteristics of becoming a man of God. As we ponder the study exercises below, let's try to focus on a vision to build godly character and a life that has significance.

PERSONAL ACTIVITIES

Read Micah 6:8 and spend time reflecting on God's will for your life. What does it mean to "do justly"? To "love mercy"? To "walk humbly with your God"?

What Christian men (or women) do you admire? Why? Are they modeling a Christlike life? Are there any biographies on these people that you can read? If so, do so! If they are still living, what can you do to get to know more about them? What in their lives can you imitate in your own life?

MENTORING ACTIVITIES

Discuss together what a man of significance looks like. What makes him significant? How is this different from being successful? Which of those traits do you see in each other?

Agree together that, in the coming week, you will each memorize Romans 12:1–2. What does it mean to "present your bodies a living sacrifice"? To not be "conformed to this world"? How does a man go about renewing his mind?

"The price of success is hard work, dedication to the job at hand, and the determination that whether we win or lose, we have applied the best of ourselves to the task at hand."

—Vince Lombardi[1]

ZEAL AND DISCOURAGEMENT

Sonny Liston was the reigning heavyweight champion of the world in the early 1960s. He was a powerhouse of a fighter, having gained the title by knocking out the previous world champ in the first round of their fight—not once, but in two successive fights. Other professional fighters were afraid of Liston, because when he landed a punch it was like getting hit by a freight train. His fights generally didn't last long for that reason, because all he needed to do was make a solid connection with his opponent's jaw, and the fight was over.

Ironically, this fact actually worked against him on the day he entered the ring against a newcomer to the sport by the name of Cassius Clay—who would later change his name to Muhammad Ali. Clay was quick and agile, but it didn't seem likely that he'd be able to stand up to the devastating punches that Liston could deliver. The world's view was that Sonny Liston was nearly invincible, and there were some sports writers who even feared that he would ruin the sport because other fighters were afraid to get in the ring with him.

But Cassius Clay was not afraid. If anything, he was brash and loud and boastful in his predictions that he would knock Liston out of the fight by the eighth round. The world mocked and laughed at Clay's braggadocio—until the fight started.

Clay danced circles around Liston. Sonny would throw one of his blockbuster punches, and Clay would simply lean back out of his reach. Liston would lunge forward for another shot and be met with a one-two combination from Clay, a tactic that would eventually become one of his trademarks. Finally, Clay's predictions became a reality, as Liston gave up and refused to enter the ring in the seventh round.

There were several factors that led to this amazing victory and defeat. First, Cassius Clay won a victory because he was faster and more agile than Sonny Liston. Time and time again, Liston threw devastating punches that Clay dodged, leaving "Big Bear" Liston swinging at the air. But this was coupled by the fact that Liston brought defeat upon himself to some extent by being overconfident before the fight. He was so convinced that Clay didn't stand a chance against his hitting power that he scarcely even bothered training for the fight. As I mentioned already, Liston was counting on the fact that his fights rarely lasted more than a few rounds because of his devastating hitting power, and he evidently anticipated that his fight with Cassius Clay would follow the same pattern. Consequently, he slacked off on his physical discipline and preparations, leaving himself no stamina when fight time came.[2]

If I were to summarize the difference between Sonny Liston and Cassius Clay in that famous boxing match, I would use one word: *zeal.* Cassius Clay had it; Sonny Liston didn't.

ZEAL FOR GOD'S KINGDOM

The word *zeal* refers to a strong, devoted passion for something. It comes from a Greek word that originally meant *heat,* and came to refer to the "warmth" or "heat" of one's passionate determination to attain some goal. A young man might pursue a woman with a heated intensity, with a strong determination that he is going to win her heart, and we would say that he is *zealous* for that woman's love.

Jesus had great zeal for the kingdom of God. He did not merely *desire* to do the will of the Father; He had a hot passion to accomplish it. He went to Jerusalem for the Passover and found people inside the temple conducting business, and in His zeal for His Father's house He made a scourge out of cords of leather, overthrew the tables, and drove men and beasts out of the temple. "Take these things away"!" He cried to the dove sellers. "Do not make My Father's house a house of merchandise!" And in that moment, His disciples remembered a verse from Psalm 69, "zeal for Your house has eaten me up" (Ps. 69:9; John 2:16).

Of course, a godly zeal will not likely call any of us to overthrow tables or drive people out with a scourge. Our zeal for God's kingdom will more often involve self-denial and undertaking difficult tasks, just as it did for most of Jesus' ministry. He was utterly determined to fulfill His Father's will, and went about teaching and healing and raising the dead—even though the religious leaders were actively working to destroy Him. This is what Isaiah was prophesying about when he wrote, "I gave My back to those who struck Me, and My cheeks to those who plucked out the beard; I did not hide My face from shame and spitting. . . . Therefore I have set My face like a flint, and I know that I will not be ashamed" (Isa. 50:6–7). Jesus' determination to obey the Father was as hard as flint; His zeal was so hot that nothing would extinguish it.

A friend recently told me about a man named George who has a great zeal for NASCAR racing. George used to be an avid fan of Dale Earnhardt, and now he just as avidly follows the races of Dale Earnhardt Jr. He managed to get his hands on a ticket to the Daytona 500 this year, and nothing was going to stop him from attending. He'd gotten the tickets at the last minute and had to scramble to make arrangements to get from the West Coast to Florida, but he discovered that airline flights were very expensive, and good connections were not available. He considered going by train, but that would have taken several days. He ended up renting a car and driving, covering almost three thousand miles in a day and a half, stopping only for gas, eating in the car, and taking a few short catnaps when he could not stay awake.

George eventually got to his seat, up in the "nosebleed" section, and settled in for a delightful day of hotdogs and excitement. And then it started to rain. It rained on and off for more than six hours, and he had not thought to pack an umbrella—but still he sat there, determined to see the race to its finish and not risk losing his precious seat. Several days later, after another grueling drive back home, my friend asked George how his trip was. "Fantastic!" he exclaimed. "My guy won!"

George paints a vivid picture of what zeal looks like. It's a passion that can almost consume us, that can "eat us up" as zeal for God's house did to Jesus. Zeal does not permit anything to get in the way of attaining its goal—not six hours of rain, not discomfort and deprivation, not expense or sacrifice, not even death, as Jesus demonstrated on the cross. Muhammad Ali had a zeal to win, and that zeal drove him to become one of boxing's greatest champions.

We all have some area in which we are zealous, and the question is, what is *yours*? You can identify an area of zeal in your life by taking note of what things you are willing to sacrifice for. Do you give up planned leisure time on the spur of the moment because your wife asks you to do yard work? Or do you willingly give up the yard work in order to play golf with friends? Your use of free time and expendable income will reveal where your zeal lies.

Our areas of zeal also show up visibly in our lives. I have a zeal for hunting and fishing. If you ever visit my home, you'll know this immediately because my walls are decorated with numerous trophies of fish and game that I've taken over the years. I had a few of my animals and fish mounted, not to show them off to my friends but because they represent to me the zeal and challenge it took to harvest that animal. Similarly, a person with a zeal for bowling will have lots of trophies and bowling paraphernalia in his home.

When you develop a zeal for God's kingdom, it will become evident in your life in the same ways. You will become eager to spend time reading His Word and praying, eager to spend time with Christian brothers and sisters, eager to turn a conversation to the meaningful things of eternity. Your home will gradually become cluttered with the things of God: Bibles, commentaries, Scripture verses, Christian music, and so forth. This does not mean that your hunting and bowling trophies will disappear, but those things will no longer be the centerpiece of your life. More than this, a home where zeal for God exists is characterized by peace, that intangible quality that has nothing to do with material possessions, and which can only come through the Holy Spirit being central in a man's life.

ZEAL IN THE MIDLIFE

As a man approaches the mid-point of his life—and beyond—it frequently happens that he finds his zeal diminishing or making a radical shift. Our culture calls this a "midlife crisis," when a man suddenly discovers that life isn't shaping up to be what he expected. It frequently occurs in men sometime during their forties or thereabouts, when they begin to take stock of what they have accomplished and where they think they're heading. This reevaluation might be triggered by some event, such as the death of a parent or loss of a job, but it can also come on more gradually, as a man slowly begins to realize that he has likely reached at least the halfway point in his life.

Some men react during this time by trying to regain their youth or by making a dramatic change in their lives, such as moving to another state or suddenly changing careers. All too often, men in this situation will try to compensate for the crisis with poor decisions, such as buying an expensive toy or suddenly dropping close friendships. And some men make devastatingly bad decisions by becoming involved in adulterous relationships or leaving their families.

But a midlife crisis is not in itself a bad thing. In fact, I would suggest that it leads to a mind-set that a man should have, as we saw when we looked at the life of Daniel in a previous chapter. He determined as a young man that he would not defile himself by disobeying the Word of God—yet sometimes the pressures and anxieties of life can cause a man who starts well to gradually lose his focus on the things of eternity and become enmeshed with the things of this world. Recognizing that your days are numbered can cause you to refocus your priorities and to reevaluate where your values truly lie.

The key to weathering the storms of midlife is to take care *not* to focus on temporal things. This includes wistful reminiscences of the past and anxiety about the gradual disappearance of youthful vigor and strength. A few years ago, there was a popular song about "glory days" that described people looking back longingly at a time that has passed—and that is precisely the thing that a godly man does not have time for. Yes, it's good to assess whether or not you have attained goals that you set when young, but only for the purpose of redirecting your energies toward the things of eternity; otherwise, such thinking leads only to discouragement and despair.

Discouragement is a very common element of midlife for many men, and this provides very fertile ground for the devil to sow seeds of despair and discontentment. One way to combat this tendency is to cultivate an attitude of gratitude, as we've discussed in previous chapters. Making a daily list of the things that God is actively doing in your life will do wonders to shift your focus away from those things that you might be disappointed about.

But there are times when the only way to overcome a midlife slump is to "keep on keeping on," to persevere in daily Bible reading and prayer simply because it's what we are commanded to do. I'm reminded of Winston Churchill's great speeches to the British people during the dark days of World War II, when he underscored the need for the people at every level to carry out their responsibilities and persevere, even in the face of apparent defeat. "We shall go on to the end . . . ," he said. "We shall fight on the seas and oceans . . . we shall fight on the beaches, we shall fight on the landing grounds, we shall fight in the fields and in the streets, we shall fight in the hills; we shall never surrender."[3]

Churchill understood the dangers of discouragement in the face of failure and setbacks, and he knew that the only way to overcome that discouragement is to press on. We must not allow past failures to dictate future behavior, and above all, we must guard against becoming apathetic and adopting a "who cares" attitude toward the important things of life.

In my experience, apathy is one of the most dangerous traps of midlife for men. When we have not attained the lofty goals we once strove for, when we have lost some of the abilities we once took for granted, and when we've already passed our glory days and don't see anything in the future but mediocrity or even outright failure and loss, we ask ourselves, "Why bother? What's the use in knocking myself out for things that I'll never accomplish? It's much more sensible just to relax and make the best of things as they are."

But God does not want His people to be apathetic about the things of eternity. He warned the church at Laodicea that their apathy was disgusting in His eyes. "I know your works, that you are neither cold nor hot," He told those believers. "I could wish you were cold or hot. So then, because you are lukewarm, and neither cold nor hot, I will vomit you out of My mouth" (Rev. 3:15–16). Apathy is the opposite of zeal; God indicated to the Laodiceans that even being *cold* toward the things of God is better than being lukewarm!

The antidote to apathy is both a spirit of thankfulness, as I've said repeatedly, and perseverance. In midlife, it's easy to become weary in well-doing, and the New Testament tells us frequently that we must be on guard against that tendency. "And let us not grow weary while doing good," Paul exhorted the Galatians, "for in due season we shall reap *if we do not lose heart*" (Gal. 6:9, emphasis added).

We lose heart for the battles of life when we focus our thinking on what might have been or on the failures of the past. When we give in to discouragement, we become like Sonny Liston in his fight with Muhammad Ali, like the boxer Paul spoke of who "beats the air" (1 Cor. 9:26). We waste all our energy in complaining and feeling sorry for ourselves, and we let our self-discipline and spiritual training slip away.

But when we determine in our hearts like Daniel that we will continue to press on, regardless of circumstances or any evident results, then we become more like a well-trained boxer who aims his punches and makes them count. This is not just true during the years of midlife; it's true throughout our lives. Daniel determined in his heart when he was young—but he undoubtedly continued to make that determination throughout his life. Being firm in our commitment to holiness is not a once-in-a-lifetime event, it's a determination that we must make over and over again, on a daily basis throughout our lives.

And remember how Sonny Liston became overconfident before his fight with Cassius Clay? He had experienced dramatic victories in the past, and he assumed that his gift of freight-train punches would bring him victory all the time—but he was wrong. Just as we cannot allow past failures or present setbacks to discourage us, so also we cannot allow ourselves to become complacent when things seem to be going well. "Therefore let him who thinks he stands," Paul warned the Corinthian Christians, "take heed lest he fall" (1 Cor. 10:12). We must take care to aim our zeal in the direction of eternity, not just once but day after day.

PERSONAL ACTIVITIES

Take some time this week to analyze where your zeal lies. For what goal have you been willing to sacrifice? What drives you to excel, and in what areas? What does it mean to have zeal for God's kingdom? How can you increase that zeal this coming week?

MENTORING ACTIVITIES

Brainstorm strategies with your mentoring partner this week on how to help each other increase your zeal for God's kingdom.

Make it a point each time you meet to deliberately encourage each other. Focus on your partner's strengths or his perseverance during difficulty, and give him encouragement to keep pressing on for God.

Hold each other accountable to spend at least fifteen minutes each day reading the Bible and praying. Also, make sure that you spend time together in prayer every time you meet.

"Do not pray for easy lives. Pray to be stronger men."
—**Phillips Brooks**[1]

JUST A LITTLE MORE

John was a young, up-and-coming salesman at a small company that had real promise for growth. His wife, Jane, had an office job across town, and the couple was very optimistic about their future. Having two lovely babies over the next five years made a few little bumps in their road, but they didn't worry—they were working hard to put away some savings, and they felt that potential problems would be covered.

Of course, John did start to notice that it was difficult to keep up with the changes in the business world. He would overcome one hurdle at work, only to discover that a taller one lay in front of him. But that's just the way of the world, he told himself. If a man wants to succeed, he needs to keep jumping those hurdles. He simply poured more energy and time into his efforts, traveled farther and for longer periods, attended more high-profile events in order to meet more potential clients. He hardly noticed that Jane was doing the same thing.

When the kids reached school age, he sometimes felt a little cheated because he couldn't remember much of their preschool years, but he reminded himself that he was working hard for their benefit. "If I can become manager," he'd say, "I'll have more time and more income for the kids. After all, I'm doing it for them." The kids became involved in a wide array of sports and extracurricular activities—no sense in going home after school, after all, since nobody was there—and this put some stress on Jane, who found herself being a chauffeur at times when she needed to be at work. But she put a "Mom's Taxi" bumper sticker on her minivan and laughed it off.

John did become manager after a few years—and he discovered that he didn't shed the problems of being a salesman; he merely inherited those problems from all the other salesmen who now reported to him. "If I can become regional manager," he said, "I'll delegate." Jane, too, had gotten a promotion, and they planned a nice party to celebrate, but something—they couldn't remember what—conflicted with the party, and they had to shrug their shoulders and move on.

A few years more, and John became regional manager. He began to delegate. His kids went off to college. His wife left him for a man who'd been paying attention to her for the past two years. He woke up one morning and realized that he wasn't even sure what his company produced anymore because most of it was made overseas. Ironically, even the financial security that he'd envisioned years before had disappeared, as he now had two college tuitions and alimony to worry about. Does this sound all too familiar? I know at least a dozen families with this scenario.

But what John didn't understand, what he'd failed to recognize throughout his career, was that financial security itself was an illusion. Rewrite that story if you'd like, and make John and Jane amazingly successful and wealthy. Maybe the tuition will no longer be a financial burden, and we can even omit the adultery and divorce. (Although, from what I've observed in my counseling experience, financial success does not lessen the likelihood of marital failure.) But even if we rewrite the story with this apparently happy ending—is the ending truly happy?

What has John gained for eternity? What has he taught his children about priorities in life or building a lasting legacy? Has he in fact loved his wife as Christ loved the church (Eph. 5:25)? The problem is that John did not understand the very basic concept of security itself: true security cannot be found anywhere but in Christ.

THE RICH FOOL

Jesus told a parable that illustrates this principle more clearly than the story of John and Jane, because He spoke about a man whose life did illustrate the attainments that the world claims will make a man secure. The story was about a very wealthy and successful man who

JUST A LITTLE MORE

had attained the pinnacle of his success in his culture. Remember that Israel was an agrarian society in which people depended upon the crops and livestock that they grew themselves.

This man owned a great deal of land, prime land that was ideal for planting and grazing.[2] Many of his neighbors had small stone huts in which they could store whatever small amounts of grain they had left over each season, and some did not even have that much, but this man had a roomy barn—in fact, he had several of them. He had been a natural businessman throughout his adult life and had reinvested profits from good crops into more land and storage facilities. He had come from a fairly ordinary background, and in our culture people would say that he had pulled himself up by his bootstraps. He was admired throughout his region for being hardworking and shrewd.

He had endured some years of drought and hardship, but he'd been careful with his money and his labors and had still been able to put away some extra for the future. Then came a year of boon crops, and his fertile fields produced an abundance that exceeded his wildest expectations.

"Finally," he said to his wife, "all our hard work has paid off! This crop will fill our barns to the top!"

Surprisingly, he found that his harvest more than filled his barns. He filled every nook and cranny in those barns and swelled the walls to the bursting point, and still he had more left over. "Well, my dear," he said to his wife, "we'll just have to tear down those barns and build bigger ones!"

"But why would we go to all that extra work?" she asked in surprise.

"Ah," he said, as though glad she'd asked, "this way, you see, we can reclaim the land that our barns are on now and plant crops there next year, and we'll buy our neighbor's field to build bigger barns on. Then I can sit back and say to myself, 'Self, you have many goods laid up for many years—you'll be well prepared for whatever unexpected surprises might come along.' And I'll sit back, take my ease, eat, drink, and be merry. I'll retire!"

But God said to him, "Fool! This night your soul will be required of you; then whose will those things be which you have provided?" (Luke 12:20).

Now, Jesus was not teaching His disciples that it is a sign of spiritual weakness to be successful. The focus of His parable was not on the fact that the man was rich—it was on the man's *response* to his success and material possessions, on his *goals* rather than on his *gains*. Another way to approach the subject is to ask ourselves the question, *when is enough enough?* The rich fool in this parable had the idea that he could secure himself against an uncertain future by laying up material possessions, and Jesus made it clear that this is the wrong way to think.

He told His disciples that the things of life are of secondary importance, while the things of eternity are of primary importance. And by "the things of eternity," I mean an intimate relationship with God. This is what Jesus meant when He spoke about being "rich toward God" rather than laying up treasure on earth. When we spend our time chasing after financial security or career success, we end up loving and coveting the things of this world. But when we deliberately pour ourselves into the kingdom of God, we grow to love Him more and more—because where our treasure is, there our hearts will be as well (Luke 12:34).

CHASING THE WIND

Now, you might be telling yourself, "I'm not trying to be successful because I love money; I'm just trying to be a responsible person." And this is not a bad thing in itself; it's important to be responsible and to pay our bills. In fact, Paul said, "If anyone will not work, neither shall he eat" (2 Thess. 3:10). But at the same time, we need to be on our guard against letting this sense of responsibility become a sense of self-sufficiency—and that is a subtle but easy change in one's attitude. With some people, the power, authority, and measure of the bank account can become an obsession in itself.

One reason for this is that pursuing financial security is like chasing the wind: it's always just a little bit ahead of you, and you can never quite grasp it. I'm reminded of the story about John D. Rockefeller, one of the richest men in American history. Someone supposedly asked him how much money was enough, and he responded, "Just a little bit more." [3]

I don't know if Rockefeller really said that, but the story still illustrates an important truth: even the richest men never reach the point where they are truly secure, because money does not bring security or joy. The very best that a man can hope for from wealth is to be comfortable throughout his lifetime—and then to die. The comfort is not guaranteed, but death is.

Please don't think I'm pretending that a man has no need of food and clothing. There are certain necessities of life, and those necessities can become even more pressing when a man has a family to provide for. But the interesting thing is that when Jesus taught this parable to His disciples, He also told them that God understands all about those necessities—and what's more, He promised that God would provide them! "For all these things the nations of the world seek after, and your Father knows that you need these things" (Luke 12:30).

This is actually very freeing news, when you think about it. Jesus was saying that He wants His followers to focus on building His kingdom, and the Father will ensure that our basic needs are met. So that leads us to our next question, which is a very important one to ask.

WHAT DOES IT MEAN TO SEEK THE KINGDOM OF GOD?

When Jesus told the parable of the rich fool to His disciples, He concluded with the moral of the story, explaining what it meant: "But seek the kingdom of God, and all these things shall be added to you" (Luke 12:31). But what does that mean?

First, we need to consider the context of the verse. Jesus was discussing the financial burdens of life, and He acknowledged that we have need of certain basic things, such as food and clothing. Furthermore, He recognized that it can sometimes be a struggle to attain these basic needs of life, that financial pressures can make a man anxious about the future. It's important to understand that He was not suggesting a lazy, lackadaisical attitude; He was not telling His disciples to be irresponsible about paying their bills.

But, on the flip side of this same coin, Jesus also was talking about the basic necessities of life, such as food and clothing. This is an important distinction in this topic—His followers need to learn to recognize the difference between providing shelter for one's family and having a bigger home in a nicer neighborhood with newer technology and a bigger mortgage. And this is a distinction we can easily forget, because when our basic needs are met, we are quick to see ways in which we can get just a little bit more—like with John D. Rockefeller. And once we become focused on that "little bit more," we are in danger of becoming like the rich fool in the parable, who had convinced himself that a little bit more would somehow give him security for the future.

The irony of materialism is that, the more we have, the more anxious we become. I can't exactly explain how this works, but I've seen it both in my own life and in the lives of others around me. More things need more upkeep, better jobs bring higher expenses, and so forth. Jesus understood this as well and repeatedly told His disciples, "Do not worry . . . do not fear . . . do not be anxious." What was His solution to those worries and anxieties? "Consider the ravens. . . . Consider the lilies" (Luke 12:24, 27). Make a deliberate effort to look for the ways in which God is meeting the needs in your life and the lives of others. This goes back to our previous topic of developing a thankful spirit, purposely taking time daily to give thanks for what God has done and is doing.

"And do not seek what you should eat or what you should drink, nor have an anxious mind" (Luke 12:29). Do not let your focus be centered on material things, and do not permit yourself to become anxious about material things. Your Father knows that you need some of them, and He has promised to provide them.

But not making material things our god is only half the equation in seeking the kingdom of God.

AND HIS RIGHTEOUSNESS

The gospel of Matthew covers Jesus' teaching on worrying about material goods, but the author adds something to what Luke tells us that Jesus said: "But seek first the kingdom of God *and His righteousness*, and all these things shall be added to you" (Matt. 6:33, emphasis added). This adds an important new dimension to seeking God's kingdom, telling us that we must simultaneously seek God's righteousness.

What is God's righteousness? Well, the answer to that question is spread throughout the Bible, which is like God's instruction manual to the human race on how to live in a righteous manner. In simple terms, seeking God's righteousness means reading His Word—and *obeying* it. Remember what James said about a man looking in the mirror and forgetting what he saw there. It is of little value to read the Bible if we fail to obey what it says.

We can certainly start our obedience with the topic that we're considering here, by constantly reordering our priorities away from material things and career success and toward other people and the things of God's kingdom. This in itself might mean some drastic changes in your life, a willingness to let go of goods or goals that might be hindering your work for the kingdom. Jesus, after all, was willing to take drastic measures in His fulfillment of God's will, even going to the cross. He told His disciples, "Sell what you have and give alms" (Luke 12:33). Now, I am not suggesting that all Christians are called to have no possessions—but I am also not suggesting that Jesus was merely being metaphorical when He said that. Sometimes, drastic measures might be called for in the pursuit of righteousness.

Seeking God's righteousness will require different things for different people at different times in their lives. But there are some basic things that remain the same at all times for all people, and that includes what Jesus said were the two most important commandments: love the Lord your God with all your heart, mind, soul, and strength; and love others as you love yourself. In a nutshell, this is what it means to seek God's kingdom and His righteousness.

And when have we acquired enough of God's righteousness? When we have just a little more.

PERSONAL ACTIVITIES

Take time over the next two weeks reflecting on God's Ten Commandments (Ex. 20:1–17). Take one command each day, meditating on what it means in your life today, and reflecting on what you need to do to obey.

When you inventory your possessions and wealth and think about the future, ask yourself, "How much is enough?" When does gaining more become also gaining more anxiety about losing what you have?

MENTORING ACTIVITIES

Make a list together of what it means to "seek first the kingdom of God and His righteousness" (Matt. 6:33). What does this mean? How is it done? What things are *not* on the list that you might otherwise be tempted to seek?

Then take that list and decide on one or two items that you will both deliberately do in the coming week.

"Wealth, like happiness, is never attained when sought after directly. It comes as a by-product of providing a useful service."

—Henry Ford[1]

MAKING A
REAL DIFFERENCE

It's not every day that I make the news, but it happened during a hunting expedition in New Zealand several years ago. Sitting at a table sipping a cup of hot coffee while I watched the sunrise through the open window, I opened the *Christchurch* morning newspaper only to find an article entitled "Copter Missing Over N. Canty." I had a hard time swallowing my gulp of coffee when I realized that this news item was about my ordeal of the night before.

I guess the blame for our predicament has to be shared with myself and the guide. We were hunting the Alpine Mountains of New Zealand for the elusive mountain goats known as *tahrs.* To find them, you have to be willing to go deep into treacherous terrain, and a helicopter is the best option to get up to the elevation where you can begin your hunt. Late in the day, our pilot set the copter down on top of a mountain to adjust some equipment—and that was when we made our mistake. In adjusting my gear, my rifle barrel inadvertently rose into the path of the rotor blade. Not only did it make a terrible sound, but the dent that I left rendered the craft unfit to fly.

What were we to do? The moonless night loomed before us with its freezing temperatures. We sent out a signal with the transponder to let anyone able to pick up the signal know that we were in a desperate situation, but the guide had little hope of a quick rescue. Instead, we would have to make our way almost five thousand feet down the rugged mountainside on foot to reach the valley floor. Our guide knew of an abandoned shepherd's hut some five to six miles north of our descent point where we could find shelter from the bitter night air. But would we be able to see well enough to navigate our way around the steep cliffs that posed such a hazard?

I had a real dilemma. With my deep-seated fear of heights, would I be able to even attempt a descent with the pilot and guide, or would it be better to try to keep from freezing to death at the nine-thousand-foot elevation with the cold temperatures? I asked the guys to help me with this decision. I told them that I didn't think I could overcome my fear of heights and that I would be better off staying alone with the helicopter. They overruled my thought and said that we had to make the descent together.

I asked the group to join me in prayer as I asked God to help guide us in the darkness and to help us overcome our fears. I felt like the psalmist who wrote, "My soul quietly waits for the True God alone; my salvation comes from Him. He alone is my rock and my deliverance, my citadel *high on the hill*; I will not be shaken" (Ps. 62:1–2, The Voice). My fully loaded utility belt had always drawn jokes from my sporting companions—but not on this night. My ammunition, knives, sharpeners, survival kit, two power bars, solar blanket, and two small penlights were just about all we had. And none of us were dressed for the difficult descent that lay before us.

I knew, as I had known so many times before, that it would take God's help to bring us through. With limited light, we began to climb down the face of the mountain. It was slow and difficult work. Once we passed the dangerous cliffs, we still had to endure thick brush that tore at our clothes and flesh. It didn't help that I had eaten very little that day due to an upset stomach, so I quickly grew more and more fatigued. On three separate occasions, I had to sit down and evaluate whether I could go on. I wanted to quit. You could say that I was paralyzed with fear. But I was buoyed by my faith in God and the encouragement and wisdom of my companions.

About 11:00 p.m. the temperature fell below freezing, but we persevered and I found myself able to draw on strength that was not my own. Cold and frightened, we finally reached the shepherd's hut and started a fire to dry out our clothing. At around 1:30 a.m., we heard the welcome sound of a helicopter, and peering out the window into the darkness of the night, we could see the searchlights of a rescue craft hovering over the general area where our helicopter was grounded. They were a good ten miles away and had little chance of discovering us if we didn't get their attention. Fortunately, one of the things hanging from my utility belt was a small beacon light. Once we turned it on, the blinking high-intensity light directed the rescuers to our doorstep. They flew us back to Queenstown where we caught a few hours' sleep before we tried to piece together the events of the previous night.

Warming my hands over my coffee cup the next morning, I set aside my newspaper and thought about the ordeal I had been through. I thought about how the peril of my situation paralleled the peril of my life before I had recognized God's love, mercy, and grace. I was truly in a hopeless situation until God reached out His hand to a young Oakland city boy to save me from sins, despair, and fears.

BARRIERS KEEPING US FROM MAKING A DIFFERENCE

Many people seeking to follow Christ's command to be His witness are challenged by meaningful tasks because of health limitations, demands of family life, or basic needs—challenges that limit a person's time, energies, and resources. That is totally understandable. But there are many of us who have the opportunities, health, and resources to get out of the foxhole and into the battle for men's souls. If we really focus on those tasks in life that have eternal significance, we can generally make the time. A very busy businessman once told me that he can always make time for something that is a priority. It is our privilege and responsibility to be used of God for His glory and purpose.

So why are there so many people not finishing well and strong? For some, it is because we are focused on the barriers or obstacles that present themselves as detours for considering God-shaped goals or visions that take us out of our comfort zone. I had to push through the barrier of my fear on the mountaintop to save my life and those with me.

FEAR CAN BE CONSUMING

One of the biggest barriers keeping us from reaching our full potential in Christ is the *fear of failure*. I've known many very successful businessmen who, when it comes to stepping outside their comfort zone, become fearful and unable to move forward with the calling upon their lives. What things frighten you? If your pastor were to ask you to lead a small group or assist tutoring some high-risk kids or meet with a guy in the church having sexual identification issues, what would be your response? What about taking a short-term mission to a third-world country? Sounds pretty scary to some.

In my own life, the fear of failure has occasionally detoured me from the challenges that were part of God's plan. I can think of times when the direction was obvious, but I let the fear of failure cripple my actions. You see, like many reading this book, my generation often heard our elders say, "don't disappoint me" or "we are counting on you to perform" or "don't be a failure." For the most part, today's younger generation has the attitude that failure is inevitable—fail quickly and try again. They don't let the fear of failure reign in their lives like my generation.

One of the greatest Bible teachers of our day is Dr. David Jeremiah, senior pastor of Shadow Mountain Community Church in El Cajon, California. I had the privilege of serving with Dr. Jeremiah as a trustee on the board of his college. Pastor David is a remarkable man who has written many powerful books, including *What Are You Afraid Of?* As I read through this book, I couldn't help thinking of how being fearful can keep us from achieving the things God desires for our lives.

Unfortunately, too many of us let our fears stand in the way of doing things that would help us finish well and finish strong. We become fearful of failure. My psychologist friends call it *atychiphobia*. The side effects and impact result in a persistent refusal to try anything new. According to David Jeremiah, "Many of the most-admired people in the Bible experience it. . . . More than two hundred people who were afraid at one time or another. Some of them were afraid of failure!"[2]

When God calls us to a task, He will also equip us for that task. Sometimes the fear of failure can get in the way of us receiving the blessings and resources that God provides to accomplish the task. "We see this consistently in the 'call narratives' of the Bible," Dr. Jeremiah continues, "those accounts in which God summons a person to a particular task. The more prominent examples are Moses, Gideon, Isaiah, Jeremiah, and Ezekiel."[3]

GIDEON'S FEAR

Gideon gives us an excellent picture of how fear can influence our lives. (You can read his story in Judges 6–8.) We first meet Gideon when he was busy threshing wheat on his father's farm—inside of a winepress! The significance of this situation might not be readily obvious to us in our modern culture, but the winepress was probably a large vat in which one crushed grapes. Farmers would thresh their wheat in the open in order to allow the breeze to carry away the chaff, the part that wasn't edible, and doing it inside a vat would have made the job far more difficult.

But we're told that Gideon was doing this unusual thing because he was afraid of the Midianites, an enemy nation that was conducting raids on the people of Israel to steal their crops and cattle. He was allowing his fear of his enemies to influence his life, making everything much more difficult. An angel of the Lord appeared to him and said, "The LORD is with you, you mighty man of valor!" (Judg. 6:12).

Now, there was a certain ironic humor in the fact that the angel addressed Gideon as a mighty man of valor, since he was cowering inside a wine vat at that moment. And Gideon revealed how deep that fear went in his response to the angel: "If the LORD is with us, why then has all this happened to us? . . . But now the LORD has forsaken us and delivered us into the hands of the Midianites" (v. 13).

The Midianites had been terrorizing the people of Israel for some time, so in that sense it is understandable that Gideon might be tempted, in a moment of discouragement, to think that he'd been abandoned by God. But the truth is that he was making a terrible—and false—accusation against God, accusing God of being unfaithful to His promises. The very fact that He had sent an angel to speak with Gideon was proof enough that He had not abandoned them.

Fear was clouding Gideon's thinking, and it was causing him to say and do things that he would probably not have said or done had he been thinking clearly. This is exactly what fear does to us: it clouds our thinking and causes us to stop trusting God. This is the reason that the Bible says over and over again, "Do not be afraid!" This is not just a casual comment like "have a nice day" or "keep your chin up." It is a command; God is telling His people, "Do not permit fear to control your attitudes and actions."

On an emotional level, fear is not volitional—that is, the emotion of fear comes upon us whether we want it to or not. That is a good kind of fear; it's the way God designed us, so that we recognize a dangerous threat and avoid it or protect ourselves. But what *is* volitional, the part that is up to us to decide, is how we respond to that fear. Gideon was experiencing fear for a legitimate reason, because the Midianites were threatening his life. But he responded by falsely accusing God, rather than by asking God to remove the threat altogether. When fear strikes our hearts, we need to voluntarily choose to turn to God for help; otherwise, the fear will lead us away from Him.

NOISE, CONFUSION, AND CHAOS CAN GET IN OUR WAY

One of the reasons I enjoy hunting and fishing so much is the isolation and peace you can find on a quiet stream, in a shady cove, or in the majestic mountains that our Lord created. With the rat-race pace of today's busy culture, it is hard to find a place where there isn't noise, clutter, confusion, and even some chaos. Even suburbia and country environments have become echo chambers for blaring televisions, radios, stereos, DVDs, CDs, tablets, cell phones, and other distracting devices. Unless we are intentional about making time to be alone with God, it is hard to find a place where the environment around us is on hold. The old expression that silence and meditation are golden is something that has become foreign to our culture.

Our Creator designed us for fellowship, peace, harmony, and reflection. There was a time in our country when the front porch on a home was more than just an architectural feature. It was a place to relax, have some meaningful discussions, and listen to God. Today many of us can't even go to sleep without some noise in the background.

I once heard about a pastor who was struggling with a number of issues and choices. There was much noise, confusion, and chaos going on in his life. He went for counsel to another more mature pastor and asked how to handle his circumstance. His mentor advised him to go out into the desert away from all the distractions of the city and pray for three days. No cell phones, no radios, nothing but what he needed to survive. The younger pastor took the advice and went into the desert. After setting up camp, he began to pray. After an hour, he was all prayed out and didn't know what to do. The next two and a half days were very difficult as he tried to settle his spirit and listen to God about his choices. The adventure improved the man's prayer life and gave him guidance on what he should do.

It is good to take the time and space to wonder about life's most important issues. This is where we get our direction, our purpose, and our heart right with God. Some of my best thoughts for books, our ministry, and our family life have come from spending some quality time meditating with my heavenly Father. Take a notebook along so you can capture those special inspirations and moments. Ask yourself questions like:

* Why was I created?

* Who am I?

* How could I experience a fuller life?

* What would I have done differently and how could I share my regrets with younger people so they can learn from my mistakes?

* If there was a fire in my house, assuming my family, pets, and Bible were already accounted for, and I could only grab three things, what would they be? What is the significance of my answer?

* What are the abilities, talents, gifts, and experiences I've used to glorify God? How could I embrace these qualities in the future to better my relationships with others?

✳ What am I missing in life that would make my life fuller?

✳ What do I want to be doing in five, ten, and twenty years? Get a piece of graphic paper and map it out.

✳ What could I do that I'm not doing now to inspire or encourage others to become givers, servers, and disciples?

✳ What would I be willing to die for?

✳ Whom can I share the above questions with that would help me identify what is realistic and periodically review my plan?

✳ What Bible verses or characters come to mind that would encourage and strengthen my faith in setting my vision, goals, and resources?

✳ When it comes to money, possessions, friends, popularity, power, and fame, how much is enough?

✳ How do I feel about my career? Is there a pathway to a job or activity I would enjoy more than what I'm doing?

✳ Am I living a balanced life (faith, work, family, leisure, private time, chores, hobbies, friendships)?

✳ What inspires me the most? How can I make time for more of that?

✳ What makes me angry, sad, or disappointed?

✳ What brings joy into my life?

✳ How can I reduce the tension in my life?

✳ What are the times (seasons, holidays, environments, etc.) that test me the most?

✳ Who are the people I most admire?

✳ Who are the people I most disrespect?

✳ What are the nonnegotiables that I believe and why?

If you take on this exercise seriously, you will begin to remove the clutter from your life (the junk in your trunk) and value the most important things, things that truly make a difference.

BALANCING LIFE'S PRIORITIES

Anyone who knows me and my driven personality would say I've been out of balance most of my life—too many responsibilities, too much work, too many ideas, too few people to help, too much desire to please others, and too little rest. While all these *too many's* have helped me accomplish much, there has been a price to pay. There have been times in my life where I felt that I did not have enough time to build deep relationships; not enough efforts in being thoughtful in my communications; limited time to enjoy the successes and victories God has allowed me to have; and most importantly not spending the amount of time with my Lord. It has only been in my later years of life that I have recognized this as a dangerous problem, and I have taken drastic steps to fix it! I now make it a point to schedule in time for building relationships. I deliberately reach out to my neighbors, inviting men to join me on fishing or hunting trips, inviting couples to join my wife and me for dinner, consciously making efforts to get to know younger men at church and inviting them into a mentoring relationship. I do this because I realize how important godly relationships are in my life, and I want to make up for lost time.

Experiencing God's peace, joy, and love comes from His divine touch upon our lives that can only be found as we deepen our relationship with Him. Like that rescue crew who found us in the darkness of a New Zealand night, God has flown into the darkness of my life to bring me out of the gravest situations. I owe everything to His mercy.

He is the One who sustains us during those times when we want to quit. He guides us when we have lost our way on the path of life. And He is ready to help those of us who are out of balance as He helped Gideon even when he didn't ask for it; as He helped me that cold, dark night on the mountain. You can bring your prayers before Him knowing that He is able to rescue even the weariest.

In my book *Wading Through the Chaos*, I discuss many of the issues we face while seeking God's perspective on life's journey. To paraphrase one of the chapters, let me conclude this chapter by stating, fear, confusion, chaos, and stress can absolutely extinguish the joy in life. They can make the healthiest person sick to his stomach. They can paralyze our ability to think clearly. Those who regularly experience these emotions know too well the by-products of fear: discouragement and doubt.

Thus, making a real difference in life, being a person of significance, isn't about doing more, being the greatest, working for the best, or building an empire. It is about seeing God's work through you to accomplish His plan and purposes while allowing us to experience His peace and joy.

PERSONAL ACTIVITIES

Make a list of the things in your life that are stealing your joy. How can these things be eliminated or changed so you can experience the peace of God? What does Psalm 34:14 mean to you?

MENTOR ACTIVITIES

What do you suppose the apostle Paul meant when he wrote Ephesians 4:8–13 about using your talents, gifts, and abilities while trusting in God to empower you?

Why is our love of God and others so important? (Matt. 22:37–40; Rom. 13:9–10; Eph. 3:19; 4:16)

"When one door of happiness closes, another opens; but often we look so long at the closed door that we do not see the one which has been opened for us."

—**Helen Keller**[1]

COPING WITH
DISCOURAGEMENT
AND FEAR

Some describe Billy Mills's 10,000-meter victory at the 1964 Olympic Games as nothing short of a miracle. During the stretch run of the last lap, he wove his way through a field of lapped runners and passed the race favorites, Rom Clarke and Mohamed Gammoudi. An Oglala Sioux Native American, Mills took up distance running while attending the Haskell Institute in Lawrence, Kansas. Later, while attending the University of Kansas and under the mentorship of Hall of Fame coach Bill Easton, he became a two-time All-American in cross country.

What motivates a man to achieve such remarkable goals? What is the force driving the mind and heart and body? At the age of eight, Mills's mother died. His father told him that his wings were broken (he was going to be handicapped without a mother) and that Bill needed to focus on a big dream. His dad encouraged Billy with these words: "It's the pursuit of a dream that heals a broken soul."[2]

If that wasn't enough, when Mills was twelve, his dad suddenly died. Heartbroken, alone, and frightened, Mills was shipped off to a school for Native Americans that would later become Haskell University. Persevering and the pursuit of challenges became his constant companions. He went out for boxing and running, but found that he could only really focus on one sport. Running with the wind became his passion.

As Billy entered college, the civil rights movement picked up and the high-court rulings directly affected him. He was treated unfairly and abused many times over. Once again, he felt alone and abandoned. The companionship of a few unbiased teammates offered him a feeling of brotherhood. They gave him confidence that provided the courage for him to pursue a beautiful young lady named Patricia who would later become his wife. She was a great inspiration and encourager to Billy.

More turmoil came into Billy's life as the college coaches treated him like a second-rate runner, asking him to "set the pace," to be the rabbit instead of being the finisher. Unfortunately, there were those who believed that Indians were quitters, people who couldn't finish anything they started. Billy quit running and gave up hope of ever becoming an athlete.

Billy recounted, "The fire to become an athlete was nearly extinguished. A few months later, Patricia said I was not the man she married. She felt the original spark to pursue my dream was still there. She placed her dreams of being an artist on hold to help me pursue my dream." Every morning she would place his running clothes and tennis shoes on the bed. Nothing was said, but one morning he looked at the clothes and decided that it was time to get back into the race.

After graduating from Kansas, he was commissioned as a second lieutenant in the Marine Corps. Billy prepared himself for the Tokyo Games knowing that he was a long shot to finish in the top positions. Unlike many of the premiere athletes, Billy trained by himself at Camp Pendleton in Southern California. His commanding officer told him that if he didn't qualify for the Olympics he'd be going to Vietnam.

He made it to the Olympics and never spoke to one reporter. All the attention was given to the top-seated athletes. In his quiet way, he lined up for the 10,000-meter run. As the starter's gun sounded, Billy began to run as never before. Halfway through the race, the old doubts that had hindered him in his college days started challenging his will to continue. He said to himself, "I will commit to running one more lap before I quit." The grueling pace challenged him physically as the desire to quit became a fear. Each time he passed by the starting line, he would challenge himself to do just one more lap.

At the beginning of the final lap, the exhausted Billy was almost elbowed off the track by another runner. That made Billy even more determined to finish strong. He suddenly reached into his heart and found new energies. His final lap times were record book stuff. Rounding the last corner he thought, "I may never be this close again—I have to do this now! Wings of an eagle! I won! I won! I won! Then I felt the finish line tape cross my chest."

After winning his gold medal, Mills turned from pursuing his own dream to helping others find their own dreams and giving back to the community that helped him reach his goals. In 1986, he helped develop a foundation for American Indian Youth called Running Strong. By bringing programs such as clean water, organic gardening, and diabetic clinics to Indian reservations, Mills won the praise of many and the recognition of a grateful nation. For his many contributions to humanity, he was awarded the Presidential Citizens Medal in 2013.

Through his many challenges and adversities, Mills chose to remain positive. His reflections of his time at the University of Kansas produce power phrases like, "Moments of hope versus doubt, joy versus sadness, success versus defeat. . . . I started to follow . . . the road of opportunity, responsibility, and accountability." It taught him that he alone was responsible for selecting the right paths for his journey to finish well and strong.

FINDING COURAGE

Sometimes it seems easier to quit when the going gets tough, as Billy Mills knew. Finishing well and finishing strong require a renewing of one's mind and spirit. This is especially true as we get older. For whatever reason, the traits of negativity can settle in on our perspective of life, leading to frustration, impatience, a lack of vision or accountability, avoidance of risk, and a limited vision of the future.

When others are telling us to quit, that is precisely the time we need to rekindle the fire within us in order to conquer doubt, fear, and the traits of negativity. Job was no stranger to criticism, but he confronted it with his great faith in God Almighty.

Then Job *reiterated his innocence*:

> **Job:** All the things from you sound the same.
> You are all terrible *as* comforters!
> Have we reached the end of your windy words,
> or are you sick *with something* that compels you to
>   argue *with me*?
> If we were to trade places,
> I could rattle on as you do.
> I could compose *eloquent* speeches as you do
> and shake my head *smugly* at you *and your problems.*
> *But I believe* I would use my words to encourage you;
> my lips would move only to offer you relief.
> And yet, *I am not you, you are not me,*
> *and my words are of no real use:*
> When I speak, my pain is not relieved;
> If I remain *silent*, it does not go away. (Job 16:1–6 The
>   Voice)

Why is it so tough to finish well and strong? We tend to focus on our own failures and inadequacies instead of the potential that God gives each one of us. Even during our worst days, the strength of the Holy Spirit within us is enough to get us through. Paul told the Christians in Rome:

> Likewise the Spirit also helps in our weaknesses. For we do not know what we should pray for as we ought, but the Spirit Himself makes intercession for us with groanings which cannot be uttered. Now He who searches the hearts knows what the mind of the Spirit is, because He makes intercession for the saints according to the will of God. And we know that all things work together for good to those who love God, to those who are the called according to His purpose. (Rom. 8:26–28)

God's Holy Spirit indwells every believer, and one of the things He does is to strengthen us when we are weak. And while He is strengthening us, He is also praying for us to the Father! He knows our deepest needs far better than even we know them ourselves, and He is able to pray in a way that no human being could do. Through the Holy

Spirit's intercession and strengthening, God the Father works all the events of our lives—even the disasters—into His plan for our good.

In *The Problem of Pain*, C. S. Lewis wrote, "God whispers to us in our pleasures, speaks in our conscience, but shouts in our pains: it is His megaphone to rouse a deaf world."[3] I have learned the hard way that pain is where our potential and destiny collide. We can't move forward without it. A big ship cannot steer a course without the engines running (our efforts) and a captain at the wheel (God in our lives). We have to trust that God is ahead of us planning the way.

DOUBTING THE POWER WITHIN US

There are numerous things that can cause us to forget or even to doubt that God's power in our lives is sufficient for all the circumstances that we face. Here are just a few of those things.

Isolation and idleness: As we draw ourselves away from those positive individuals who can comfort us, we allow our minds to doubt and fear. As we saw in the life of Trudy Ederle, it is very important to have people in our lives who will encourage us and spur us on toward godliness. Another aspect to this problem is the fact that we can become lazy when we don't have mentors in our lives who challenge us to greater levels of holy living. This laziness can lead to idleness, not merely spending our time in worthless pursuits, but even simply adopting a "why bother?" mentality in spiritual matters. As the old saying goes, the devil finds work for idle hands.

Low self-image or inflated self-image: Paul tells us in Romans 12:3 that a man is "not to think of himself more highly than he ought to think, but to think soberly." This does not mean that we are to think of ourselves as worthless, for that would be false. Jesus' willingness to die on our behalf proves that we are of great value in the eyes of God. But our world is constantly telling us that we should have high self-esteem and strive to love ourselves, and this teaching is contrary to the Word of God. When we "think soberly" about who we are, we come to a proper balance of understanding that all men are of great value to God, while also recognizing that we are of no greater value than our next-door neighbors. We are to be neither negative nor haughty in our spirit about our value before God and others.

Pride: Scripture tells us that Lucifer grew proud when he said in his heart, "I will be like the Most High"—and for that sin, he was cast out of heaven (Isa. 14:12–14). He then carried that poisonous pride to Eve, deceiving her into believing that she could "be like God" by eating what God had expressly forbidden (Gen. 3:5). The irony is that Adam and Eve already were like God, but following the advice of the evil one led to the human race becoming *less* like God. Pride can cause a man to destroy the very things in his life that led him to become proud in the first place.

Unconfessed sin: Unless we daily ask God to forgive us of our sins and to give us the power to conquer our sin, we cannot be successful. Notice, however, that I do not say "if we sin," because I already know that we all *will* sin (1 John 1:10). None of us will be set free from the struggles of the flesh until we are eternally set free from the flesh itself, and that will not happen as long as we occupy the flesh in this world. But the good news is that "if we confess our sins, He is faithful and just to forgive us our sins and to cleanse us from all unrighteousness" (1 John 1:9). If we are to finish well and strong, we must make a habit of keeping short accounts with God. When we commit sin, we must immediately confess it and get back into righteous living.

Forgetting that you are a role model: Every one of us is a role model. We might not recognize it, but somewhere there is someone who is watching your life and learning what it means to be a godly man—from you! So the question is not, "Am I a role model?" The question is, "What kind of role model will I be?" If we remind ourselves frequently of this responsibility, we will be more likely to remember that our words, actions, and attitudes are influencing people around us. This also ties back to Paul's injunction to "think soberly" (Rom. 12:3), as it is a sobering responsibility to be modeling Jesus to the world around us.

Refusal to forget the past and move on to the future: The devil loves to get us stuck in the boxing ring, beating ourselves up over past failures or sin. What's even worse, sometimes the devil doesn't have to urge us to this self-defeating boxing match—we will do it ourselves because it somehow makes us feel self-righteous. This is twisted thinking, but we all fall into it from time to time. But past failures and sin are exactly that—past—and there is nothing we can do to change the past. God wants us to let go of the past and pay attention to the present, always keeping our eye on the eternal future.

Coping with struggles and pain: When we find ourselves faced with circumstances beyond our control, our natural impulse is to think that God has abandoned us, or He's punishing us for something. It is good to assess our lives at such times to see if we are living with unconfessed sin or harboring an unrepentant spirit, for God does discipline His children as our perfect Father. But the bigger picture is that when we strive to become like Christ, we are destined to suffer like Christ. Jesus warned His disciples of this fact repeatedly: "And you will be hated by all for My name's sake. But he who endures to the end will be saved" (Matt. 10:22). One cannot be great without failures and pain. The more failures, pain, and suffering you experience, the deeper your convictions can become.

Run the Race to Win. Billy Mills gives us a good example of what it means to cope with discouragement and fear. Here are some basic lessons that we can glean from Scripture, illustrated by the determination of Mills.

Bad things happen, even to good people. As I've already said, Jesus warned His disciples that suffering is part of growing to become like Him. Bad things are going to be part of life; that's just a guarantee. What's important is not what circumstances come into our lives, but what we do with them. You can use the bad things that have happened in your life to join the ranks of quitters, or you can use them as stepping-stones to strengthen your character and to build a legacy that will encourage those around you. When bad things happen, we are called to persevere just the same.

> For our light affliction, which is but for a moment, is working for us a far more exceeding and eternal weight of glory, while we do not look at the things which are seen, but at the things which are not seen. For the things which are seen are temporary, but the things which are not seen are eternal. (2 Cor. 4:17–18)

Don't quit just because those around you don't believe in you. You are a child of the King. People are fickle, and we must be careful not to care more about what others think than what God thinks. People can take your money, reputation, position, power, possessions, and citizenship, but they can't take your faith or your power to choose. Choose to not be distracted from your mission by those who wish you to fail.

> The Spirit Himself bears witness with our spirit that we are children of God, and if children, then heirs—heirs of God and joint heirs with Christ, if indeed we suffer with Him, that we may also be glorified together. (Rom. 8:16–17)

Focus in on your goals, plans, and purpose to stay centered. As you focus there will be those who will try to knock you off the track: an elbow to your ego, a hand temporarily stopping your dreams, a foot that crushes your spirit, or someone who spits on your reputation. Hang in there and don't let a temporary change in your direction throw you off the track. If God gave you a vision, then pursue it until he clearly takes that objective off the table:

> Not that I have already attained, or am already perfected; but I press on, that I may lay hold of that for which Christ Jesus has also laid hold of me. Brethren, I do not count myself to have apprehended; but one thing I do, forgetting those things which are behind and reaching forward to those things which are ahead, I press toward the goal for the prize of the upward call of God in Christ Jesus. Therefore let us, as many as are mature, have this mind; and if in anything you think otherwise, God will reveal even this to you. Nevertheless, to the degree that we have already attained, let us walk by the same rule, let us be of the same mind. (Phil. 3:12–16)

Sometimes a goal or dream looks so far away that it seems impossible to reach. Billy Mills tried to stay focused on the immediate goal before him to finish one more lap. When we try to visualize completing a major project, it feels overwhelming. For me, it was taking on an assignment to write five books in fifteen months. But a word at a time begins to make up a sentence. A number of sentences make up a chapter. Several chapters make up a book of fifty thousand words. In other words, a long journey is only accomplished one step at a time. Don't be overwhelmed by how far you have to go; just concentrate on completing this one step—but keep your eyes focused on the goal of finishing well and strong.

God promises us that He is with us and will not fail us. As the apostle Paul put it, "But none of these things move me; nor do I count my life dear to myself, so that I may finish my race with joy, and the ministry which I received from the Lord Jesus, to testify to the gospel of the grace of God" (Acts 20:24).

PERSONAL ACTIVITIES

Which of the following things do you see in your life at present? What is causing them? What can you do to change those circumstances?

* ✱ Frustration

* ✱ Impatience

* ✱ A lack of accountability

* ✱ Avoidance of risk

In the past experiences of your life, when has God allowed suffering or hardship to affect you? What things did you learn from those experiences? In what ways did they affect your character? In what ways were they similar to the sufferings of Christ?

MENTORING ACTIVITIES

Over the coming month, do a Bible study together on the book of Job. What sort of man was Job? What trials in his life were beyond his control? What things did he have control over? How can he be a role model in times of hardship?

*"I'm convinced more than ever that man finds
liberation only when he binds himself to God
and commits himself to his fellow man."*

—President Ronald Reagan [1]

WHAT MAKES **ME**
ME

Robert was an older man in my church when I was young. I knew
him because he was always at church, no matter when I went there.
Bible study, youth group, Sunday worship, special events—you name
it, Robert was there. He was one of those guys who's always busy in
the background of things, always there unobtrusively working away
emptying the garbage, sweeping the floor, tidying up the pews, fixing
things. He was an electrician by trade, and I learned later that he had
single-handedly done most of the wiring and electrical work in our
building years before.

One day, I found him repairing a light in the men's room, and
I thought I'd make a little joke. "Gee, Robert," I said with a smile,
"you're a regular 'fixture' in this place aren't you!" He laughed at the
pun, but then he suddenly grew serious.

"You know," he said, putting down his tools, "I wasn't always busy
with God's work." He looked at me for a moment, but I let him finish.
"I used to play golf."

Now that comment really piqued my curiosity. He made it sound
like playing golf and serving God were mutually exclusive, and I simply didn't understand what he meant. But I handed him his pliers and
helped him finish fixing the light fixture, and he began to tell me
about his earlier years.

It wasn't that playing golf in itself was a bad thing, he explained; it
was his attitude toward golf that was a problem. Robert had done more
than just "play golf." He'd been a golf addict. This sounded funny to
me at first. I mean, how bad can it be to be "addicted" to playing golf?

But as he unfolded the story, I slowly began to realize that he didn't find it the least bit amusing.

He would play golf nearly seven days a week, sometimes playing two or three rounds in a day. How can a man do that, I asked, and still hold a job? By working extra hard and efficiently, he said—but not to do a good job; merely to get away to the course. He told me with a sad laugh about the time he'd invented an excuse to his boss for why he had to leave early—then actually saw his boss later playing a round on the same course! (He hid behind a tree to avoid discovery.)

In those days, a round of golf was less expensive than it is these days, but it was still a costly habit for Robert. Greens fees really add up when you play almost daily, and there was also the cost of "needing" better equipment, a need that somehow never goes away, as we discussed in an earlier chapter. He would also take weeklong vacations with golfing buddies, traveling to more prestigious courses around the country—around the world, nearly, as he once played St. Andrews in Scotland.

As with most addictions, the ones who suffered most were his family. He would spend most Saturday mornings at the course, coming home around noon or so to do household chores, then rushing off for another afternoon round. He squeezed golf around his work schedule for the sake of his job, which meant that he had to sacrifice his family schedule for the sake of golf. He told me that he played golf during his honeymoon, and reminisced with another sad laugh about the time he built a sandbox for his kids—then used it to practice his sand-trap strokes.

Our culture uses the phrase "golf widow" in a humorous way, but Robert said that it was no joke in his house. He had all but abandoned his wife, at least as far as his availability to her, "in order to walk around smacking a silly little ball in the grass," as he put it.

And then he gave his life to Christ—and that brought about some sudden changes in his life. He became a Christian in his thirties, as I recall, and was almost immediately convicted that his priorities were all wrong. As he grew in his understanding of Scripture, Robert began to pour his life and energies into his family and his relationship with God, and soon the zeal he'd felt toward golf was redirected into the kingdom of God. I'll never forget attending his funeral years later when I was in my twenties, and listening to the testimonies of a life well spent for Christ. Our pastor said in his eulogy, "Robert burned himself out in service to God."

REDIRECTING OUR ZEAL

In a previous chapter, we discussed the topic of zeal for the kingdom of God, and Robert illustrated genuine zeal throughout his life. As a young man, he'd had a tremendous zeal to play golf, but in his midlife, he redirected that zeal into the things of God. Everyone has some area of zeal simply because we naturally get excited when we discover something that we're really good at. This is especially true of men, as God made us with an inborn drive to excel and succeed. The passion that fires up the moment we discover an area where we can excel is a natural indicator of a God-given gift.

David praised God because he was "fearfully and wonderfully made" (Ps. 139:14) as he reflected upon the ways in which God had designed him. David knew that God had given him certain skills and gifts, and his life certainly reflected those gifts. He was a great leader of men, a skilled tactician in war, a mighty fighter who was able to slay lions and bears, even a gifted poet and songwriter. David served God throughout his life by tapping into those gifts and using them to serve God.

Robert was a skilled electrician, and he used that skill in service to our church when he completely revamped the electrical and lighting systems. But he also was gifted with boundless energy, one of those people who always seems to be fired up and eager to get going. He had once poured that energy into golf, but later he redirected it into service to the Lord.

Now, you might be thinking, *Well, Robert merely replaced his golf addiction with a "work-at-the-church" addiction—the end result was the same, spending time away from home.* And that is a valid consideration. There is a danger of turning almost anything into an excuse to avoid things that one doesn't want to address, and I have known men who used church responsibilities as an excuse to avoid being responsible at home. Robert was not like that, simply because he had a gift for needing little sleep and was able to pour himself into his family with the same gusto that he had for church projects.

But it is a danger that a man needs to guard against, just the same. The key is to remember that serving others is a central feature of serving God, and that service needs to begin with those people who are closest to us. Robert served his wife and children faithfully and first, using his leftover energies to serve around the church and community.

And, as I said already, one of the best ways to serve others is by doing the things we do best.

FEARFULLY AND WONDERFULLY MADE

God designed the human body so that every part of the body has a specific role to play—and every part is specifically designed to fulfill that role. For example, the eardrum is designed to reverberate when sound waves hit it, enabling us to hear the world around us. But a person can't tell what color a car is when he hears its horn—he needs his eyes for that, because the eyes are designed to respond to light rather than sound waves. A person functions best in life when all his body parts are functioning correctly, doing the jobs they were designed to do.

In the same way, we can best serve the body of Christ by doing the things that God has uniquely designed us and prepared us for. Just as He created every part of our body for a specific purpose, so also He has created and prepared each one of His children for a specific form of ministry within the body of Christ. The important thing is for each of us to find that ministry and function within it with all our might.

I have a close friend named Carman who has struggled with a degenerative disease since her teen years. By the time she was in her mid-twenties, she used a wheelchair full-time. Today, in her fifties, she can barely lift her arms to feed herself as the disease slowly causes the muscles to waste away and stop functioning. She has also undergone some very traumatic tragedies in her life, including violence and worse, while lacking any ability with which to defend herself. Most people would be bitter and discouraged about life had they undergone even a portion of what she has endured.

But not Carman. She has remained determined all her life to focus on the things that God has given her rather than on the things that He has withheld, and to use those gifts to serve Him as fully as her frail body will allow. She has worked for years with Joni and Friends, a Christian organization that ministers to people with disabilities, mentoring other women with disabilities. She recently completed a rigorous master's degree program in Christian counseling, specifically so that she could more effectively serve others who want to follow Christ.

"God never makes mistakes," she'll frequently say. "We need to not focus on our *in*abilities and try to discover our *unique* abilities. He might allow tragedy to touch our lives, but He is always in control—and He is always good."

Your unique abilities encompass much more than just the things you're good at. God uses every event of our lives to shape and refine who we are, to better equip us to serve His body. Robert had training and skills as an electrician, and he was able to use those skills in ministry. Carman, on the other hand, is severely limited in her physical skills because of her health, yet she has been through things that most of us will never experience—and God has used those experiences to shape her in a way for unique fields of service that nobody else could fill.

"NOT ME, LORD!"

Sometimes, however, it can be difficult to get a realistic picture of how we are unique and different from everybody else. It's easy to become a spectator in life because of this, to sit back and say, "I don't really have anything to offer that someone else can't do better." This can become a trap, because we can get quite comfortable with our lives as they are and never take any risks to try something new—and, consequently, never accomplish great things for God's kingdom.

Moses illustrated these principles very clearly. His life began during a time when the pharaoh of Egypt made a decree that all male babies were to be killed. His mother put him in a straw basket and floated him into some reeds on a river, and it so happened that Pharaoh's own daughter came along and found him. Now that in itself would be seen as an amazing coincidence in human terms, but God had a plan for Moses before Moses was even born, and He was working out all the events and details of His future servant's life in order to prepare him for a job that He had in mind.

So Moses was adopted by Pharaoh's daughter, and she brought him up in Pharaoh's house. He was raised in the courts of the world's most powerful king, in the center of the world's greatest nation. He had the best and most advanced education that could be obtained, and was trained in every art and science by the world's best teachers. Perhaps a modern equivalent might be to be adopted by the queen of England and brought up in Buckingham Palace, being sent to Oxford and Cambridge and trained for a career in Parliament.

For this was Moses' experience, and he was undoubtedly groomed for future leadership as a member of Pharaoh's court. He would have been trained in the law and judicial matters, taught how to settle disputes as a judge and how to take charge and command men. As a young man, he might have anticipated a career in Egypt as a right-hand man to the pharaoh himself, and probably had visions of a future of wealth and prestige in the world's greatest nation.

But then an unexpected event happened in his life. He was out walking and he came upon a Hebrew slave being beaten by his Egyptian master, and something stirred inside Moses' heart. He suddenly remembered that he, too, was a Hebrew, and he found himself feeling great compassion for the plight of the Israelites. He didn't know it, but that compassion was the stirring of God's Holy Spirit, creating in him a heart that moved to the same things that moved God's heart.

Moses reacted in a bad way and murdered the Egyptian, reminding us that Moses was a real man who was capable of great sin, just as all of us are. He was not some kind of superman; he was made of the same flesh and blood as the rest of us. Yet God used even this great sin to move His purpose forward, and Moses was forced to break all his ties with Egypt and flee to another nation.

One day he was sitting near a well in a foreign land where he did not know anybody. He probably was thinking inside, *Well, I've made a colossal mess of things! What am I going to do now? How could God ever use me, after what I've done?* Perhaps he wasn't even thinking of God at all. But at that moment, a group of girls came along to water their sheep at that well, and while Moses watched distractedly, some rough shepherd men came up and pushed the girls away, refusing to allow them access to the well. Moses intervened, this time without violence (we can assume that he had learned a lesson from that failure), and eventually gained a wife in the process.

He moved in with the father of those girls and married one of them, living with his in-laws and working as a lowly shepherd—for the next forty years! This was the man who had been destined for great things in the court of the most powerful king on earth, now wandering through the wilderness leading a flock of ornery sheep day after day. What a hopeless failure his life had turned out to be.

And that was when God came to him at the burning bush. His conversation with God is worth looking at, because it reveals his all-too-human heart. God told him to go back to Pharaoh and ask him to let the Israelites go. Moses' response was natural: "Who am I to do such a thing?" Perhaps he was remembering that he was a wanted man back in Egypt, a fugitive murderer who would be arrested on the spot if he returned. God assured Moses that He would be with him through it all and gave him two dramatic miracles as signs that He meant what He said.

But Moses held back because of his inadequacies. "Look," he said, probably shuffling his feet in nervousness, "I'm not eloquent [which wasn't true], and I talk real slow [which might have been], and you haven't miraculously fixed *that* in spite of these other two miracles!" This last part was merely trying to blame God for his own disobedience, but God's response to Moses' fears is very important for us to understand: "Who has made man's mouth? Or who makes the mute, the deaf, the seeing, or the blind? Have not I, the LORD? Now therefore, go, and I will be with your mouth and teach you what you shall say" (Ex. 4:11–12).

God had been preparing Moses all his life for a specific calling, equipping him for a job that nobody else could do. Yet Moses was not aware of that throughout his life; he was around eighty when God met him at the burning bush, and he probably thought that he'd had his only shot at doing anything significant, that life was pretty much a done deal and there were not going to be any more opportunities for him to do something new.

But God had also been preparing that job for Moses, creating a unique space that only Moses could fit into exactly. The man and the job were crafted in the same shape, so to speak. Even Moses' past sin had been covered over by God, and the men who wanted to arrest him had all died off.

Moses tried to dodge his calling by pointing out his inadequacies, but God pointed out how he had been specifically prepared for that calling—while at the same time *not* removing his inadequacies. "I will teach you what to say," God told him. "I'm even going to use your inadequacies so that you and others can see that it is My power at work, not yours."

God uses the events of your life to shape you into a unique child of Christ, and at the same time He is also busy creating a space for you to fill that is shaped for a perfect fit to who you are. He can even use past failures for His glory—but He requires that we first be willing to obey.

PERSONAL ACTIVITIES

Take eight sheets of blank paper, lined or unlined as you like, and label each sheet with one of the following categories. Then spend the next week filling in what aspects of your character, personality, and life experiences illustrate or define each category. If you're married, be sure to ask your wife's input on each as well.

Faith: How long have you been a Christian? How would you rate your level of Scripture knowledge: deep, medium, superficial?

Church: What ministries does your church have available, both for participation and leadership opportunities? Does it offer missions opportunities, at home or abroad?

Spiritual gifts: Prayerfully read and meditate on 1 Corinthians 12. Do an assessment of where your own spiritual gifts might lie. Seek input from others who know you well. There are many books available for further study on this topic, such as *Ministering Through Spiritual Gifts* by Dr. Charles Stanley. Or try an online test, such as http://www.spiritualgiftstest.com.

Natural Talents: What sort of things do you do well? This can be anything that you're good at; don't worry if you think it has no practical application—just get it down on paper and let God lead in ways that you can use your talents.

Personality Type: Do you tend to be outgoing (extroverted) or quiet and reflective (introverted)? Do you prefer to focus on a task, or on other people? Do you prefer to be creative and invent your own design, or to follow a specific set of steps with a clear goal? There are many resources available for further information on this category, and I recommend *Spirit-Controlled Temperament* by Tim LaHaye (Tyndale, 1993).

Team Playing Style: Are you more comfortable being a leader or a follower? Do you like to manage others closely in a project, or do you prefer to let others do what they do best? If you had to choose to play a team sport (e.g., baseball or basketball) or a solo sport (e.g., golf or tennis), which would you choose?

Passions: What gets you fired up with enthusiasm? If you had an entire weekend all to yourself with no obligations, what would you do? If there were only one thing that you could accomplish in your life, what would it be?

Life-Shaping Experiences: What events or experiences in your life so far have been most significant? What milestones can you point to as places where your life or outlook changed permanently? What aspects of your life today are results (direct or indirect) of experiences or events in childhood or teen years?

MENTORING ACTIVITIES

Ask your mentoring partner to do the personal assessment activity above on his own, then spend time going over your assessments together. Help each other see things that you've missed or fine-tune things you've written. Pray together over the coming month that the Lord would show you both how to use your gifts, skills, and experiences in service to Him. Read 1 Corinthians 12 and sort through some ideas about your spiritual gifts.

WHAT MAKES ME ME

Have you spoken with your pastor, close friends, or family and asked them to evaluate your natural and spiritual gifting?

Spend time together discussing your past passions (e.g., fishing, hunting, golfing, photography, etc.). Did they consume you, or was there balance in your life for faith, family, and friends? What things got you fired up when you were younger? Do they still excite you today? If not, why not? How might you redirect past zeal into a renewed passion for things of God?

If you knew that you had a month to live, what would be your priorities? How would life change—one more fish, one more animal trophy to take, one more round of golf to play, or more time interacting with family and seeking God's plan for your life?

IT'S **TIME** TO JUMP

The 2013–14 NFL football season was packed with many great memories. While it was not a big surprise that the San Francisco 49ers beat the Carolina Panthers in the second round of the NFC playoffs by a score of 23–10, no one watching the game will ever forget one very special play. The Panthers had driven down to the 49ers' one-yard line and it was now fourth down. The 49ers coaches had predetermined to switch up their goal line defense and place six-foot-three, 259-pound Pro Bowl outside linebacker Ahmad Brooks into the unfamiliar position of inside linebacker, thus going for a modified 5-3 look.

Trying to anticipate the count before the ball was snapped, Ahmad prematurely jumped over the center and tackle, flying through the air, and barely came into contact with Panthers quarterback Cam Newton. Because the ball was so close to the goal line, the penalty ended up only being a half yard, and it didn't really affect the game, as the 49ers eventually took over on downs. Newton's delayed flop (dramatized fall over on his backside) even further highlighted the unusual demonstration of Ahmad's pent-up energy that led to a launched linebacker taking out his emotions on an unprepared quarterback.

PLAYING IT SAFE

For years, Don Davis had dreams about following in the footsteps of his position mentor Tedy Bruschi. He had watched Tedy jump over the offensive line many times, nailing the quarterback before he could hand the ball off or throw a pass. As a backup linebacker, Don had practiced that move and rehearsed it in his dreams. When the call comes from the defensive coach for a "Mike Blitz" in the A Gap (between the center and the tackle), it is an opportunity for the middle linebacker to show what he is made of. The problem is that if you hesitate at all on the move, you could get nailed by a halfback. Being suspended in the air and having a 250-pound halfback hit you isn't exactly a good thing.

Don said, "The day finally came when I was on the field and the coaches called a 'Mike Blitz.' I had the opportunity but, just as I was getting ready to jump, I saw the halfback move into the gap. Instead of a complete jump, I sort of did a step-aside on one foot to miss the half-back. By the time I got to the quarterback, the pass had been thrown. I missed the opportunity to apply what I have been trained to do."[2]

IT'S TIME TO JUMP

Theodore Roosevelt was one of our most admired presidents. He had a passion and level of commitment that few men display. During one of his many inspirational speeches, he remarked:

> Far better it is to dare mighty things, to win glorious triumphs, even though checkered by failure, than to rank with those poor spirits who neither enjoy much nor suffer much, because they live in that grey twilight that knows neither victory nor defeat.[3]

We can never experience greatness or be a person of true significance if we are always playing it safe. As we grow older, we tend to take fewer chances—and, in many ways, that is a good thing. If we all acted like we did when we were teenagers, not many of us would grow old enough to talk about matters such as this.

As we read about the lives of the disciples of Jesus Christ and how they were willing to jump into their faith, we stand in awe of their courage, passion, persistence, perseverance, dedication, and sacrifice. Is there something keeping you from being a devoted person of God? Are you hesitant about discussing matters of eternal significance? Some people are petrified when thinking about the issues of sacrifice. What about you?

I remember a time when the family of a dying friend of mine called me to be by his side. After he breathed his last breath, I sat down with the family to see what I could do to help them through the next days and weeks. As their pastor, I was honored to be part of the conversation on such matters. Unfortunately, no one was prepared to have the discussion about the arrangements necessary for a proper burial and memorial service. Beyond the most important eternal issues, death and dying was something the family had not discussed.

And for many of us, issues that are foreign or scary are not things that we want to think about. That is pretty normal. But the apostle Paul reminded us that "I can do all things through Christ who strengthens me" (Phil. 4:13). So we are encouraged to not only finish but to finish well and strong. Don't let the shadow of age detour your desire to get out into the light of new experiences and to journey through the unknown.

In Matthew 14:25–30, we read an account of Peter who trusted Christ enough to *jump in*. It was in the middle of the night, pitch dark in the center of the Sea of Galilee, and Peter was in a boat with some of the other disciples. Suddenly, they saw someone walking toward them—walking on the water! But in the midst of their terror, they heard the voice of Jesus calling out, "Be of good cheer! It is I; do not be afraid." And then Peter did something incredible: he asked Jesus to let *him* walk on the water too! As you already know, no sooner had he gotten almost to Jesus than he was overcome with fear and began to sink.

What was it that caused Peter to sink? He took his eyes off Jesus and looked at the waves. What causes us to have moments when our faith is weak, when we feel like we are sinking under the weight of life's problems, or when things just go in the wrong direction? We look at the situations that the wave currents of life create. We focus on the negative thinking and circumstances that cause our knees to knock.

TODAY I'M GOING TO JUMP IN

One of the mind-sets that separates those who finish well and strong is a desire to jump in and to be determined in tackling new challenges, adventures, or ways to serve our Lord. According to my friend Don Davis, to be an All-Pro linebacker or successful in life you need to take *authority* over your mind. God gave us authority over our circumstances and the things we need to subdue. When He created Adam, God gave him authority "over every living thing that moves on the earth" (Gen. 1:28), and that assuredly included the thoughts of his own mind! Taking authority over our thoughts means that we need to take charge of what we think, not simply let our minds wander as though they had a will of their own.

In the book of Romans, Paul tells us that we need to be transforming our minds (Rom. 12:2); we need a new way of thinking, a new attitude. If our focus is on our sin nature or negative thinking, we are being robbed of the joy and peace that God intended. Remember, the devil and negative thinking are like a thief who comes to steal, kill, and destroy our present and future joy (John 10:10). Our determination to "jump in" has less to do with our abilities and more to do with God's strength and blessings upon our lives. We need to have the right attitude.

ARE YOU WILLING TO BE OBEDIENT?

If our minds are right, then we need to check out our motives. Are we willing to be obedient? Being obedient means playing our position, and playing it well. Ahmad Brooks, the linebacker who jumped over the opposing blockers in the game against the Panthers, is a powerful and skilled player with lots of potential, but he jumped over the line before the ball had been snapped. The coaches had placed him in a situation where he did not recognize the rules of the game; he was out of his proper position; and he could have cost his team the victory.

We also need to be *quick* to obey, willing to take risks for God's kingdom when He calls us to do so. Don Davis had a chance at carrying out a memorable play in the style of his own mentor and hero. But when that opportunity came, he hesitated because of the team's opposition, and he missed his chance. God in His grace does give second chances when we fail—and third and even more—but our goal is to be responsive to the leading of His Spirit and to obey His Word quickly and eagerly.

Being obedient doesn't imply that we won't have problems. On the contrary, if we are obedient, we will definitely have trials. Going the extra mile to be that significant person and to make eternal differences will mean, like Ahmad and Don, that we find ourselves facing strong opposition, and sometimes needing to be patient.

So, why not simply play it safe—just sit at home, read your newspaper, and enjoy some hobbies? Solomon wrote, "A man who isolates himself seeks his own desire; he rages against all wise judgment" (Prov. 18:1). Solomon's insight suggests that when we decide to sit on the bench and let others carry the ball of God's Word, we are actually indulging in selfish desires. By sitting back and letting others do the work of God's kingdom, we are being self-indulgent, and we are expressing contempt for those who are actually doing the work that we refuse to help with.

Some people, out of selfishness, avoid relationships or conflict with others. Their self-centeredness makes them enemies of sound judgment, refusing to recognize that with opportunity comes risk, and with risk comes potential for pain—but with pain comes the possibility for personal growth, and with personal growth comes the chance to know God and make Him known.

NOT WHO WE ARE BUT WHOSE WE ARE

We are privileged! It matters little about your occupation, credentials, physical fitness, age, beauty, or financial success. Those are things that can describe who we are. But what really matters is that we understand and appreciate the privilege of *whose* we are. We are children of the King. We are His creation. We are chosen and privileged. We are equipped to jump in.

Some of us feel that the battles of life have taken the fight out of us. We feel too whipped to be equipped or to be of any use to God. My friend, God is the equipper. We are responsible to be obedient, at peace, and to have a heart to do the things of the Lord. But the evil one whispers in your ear that you are too old, not educated enough, too shy, too sinful, and so on. We must remember that we are children of the King of kings and that the battle is the Lord's (2 Chron. 20:15). And when it comes to being too old, let's remember that Abraham was over one hundred when Isaac was born (Gen. 21:5); Moses was over eighty when he led the children of God out of Egypt (Ex. 4:18–7:7); Noah was six hundred years of age when the flood waters came (Gen. 7:6). Think you are too old to do something for God? God is not as much interested in your age as He is in your availability.

God is continually seeking after those who are willing to "stand in the gap" (Ezek. 22:30). You are the apple of His eye (Ps. 17:8) and He will use you as long as you are willing and obedient to Him.

As Scripture tells us, a Christian's life is "hidden with Christ in God" (Col. 3:3). That means that nothing can touch our lives—nothing whatsoever—unless it first touches Christ! This is more than simply a matter of whom we belong to; it is a matter of in whom are we hidden. Jesus has us safely encompassed with His almighty arms. Our physical age has nothing to do with what we can accomplish, because we can accomplish all things only through Him who holds us.

HOW CAN WE JUMP IN?

How can you feel comfortable about jumping into the calling or leading that God has put on your heart so that you can finish both well and strong? My friend, you aren't alone. God has given you the desire to pursue a dream, to make your life count for eternal things, to build a lasting legacy. He has also given you a real helper: the Holy Spirit (John 14:16–17).

Very few of us like change. We enjoy comfort and we like things to be the way we want them. That is one of the things that makes "jumping in" a challenge. This is one of the places where we exercise faith. If you believe that God is asking you to do something for His kingdom, He is also asking you to increase your faith. Several times in the New Testament, Jesus told His disciples that they had "little faith" (e.g., Matt. 8:26; 14:31). Yet He also told His disciples that all they needed was just a little faith (Matt. 17:20) and they could do great things. How is your faith in God and what He has called you to do? Perhaps it is to start a new ministry in your church or to strengthen your marriage or to figure out a way to spend more time with your family or to change jobs. If you truly believe He has called you to this, you have to take the first step and trust Him to work out His plan through you.

When the children of Israel were about to enter the promised land (Josh. 3), the river Jordan was at flood stage. The Levites, carrying the ark of the covenant, were to be the first ones to cross the river. They had to put their feet into the raging, flood-swollen waters before the river Jordan would part and they all would pass over on dry land.

The Jordan did not part its waters until *after* the Levites stepped in (v. 13)! Certainly their faith was strengthened through that experience, and your faith will also be strengthened when you "put your feet in the water." So, is it time for you to jump in?

WHEN WE JUMP IN WE NEED THE SUPPORT AND ACCOUNTABILITY OF OTHERS

Don Davis did not take the jump into a huge offensive line by himself. He received the play from his coaches; his teammates knew what he was going to do, and they were ready to help him charge the quarterback. Each team member had his assignment. According to Christ, we are more than just a team. We are a body—the body of Christ (1 Cor. 12). As the body, we are to care for one another, support one another, and treat one another with love and kindness. When we act as the "body" or "the church," we are affirming one another in our endeavors. We pray for one another, and we pray for God's direction in one another's lives.

If we don't have the accountability of others, we can quickly find that our battles turn into wars. We need one another. No one would start to build a house without the help of others—the person with the building supplies, an architect, and others to help. The same is true when making a life-changing decision. We rely on mentors, pastors, friends, and family to talk with us and pray with us.

In writing to the Christians in Ephesus, the apostle Paul wrote, "Finally, my brethren, be strong in the Lord and in the power of His might. Put on the whole armor of God, that you may be able to stand against the wiles of the devil. For we do not wrestle against flesh and blood, but against principalities, against powers, against the rulers of the darkness of this age, against spiritual hosts of wickedness in the heavenly places. Therefore take up the whole armor of God, that you may be able to withstand in the evil day, and having done all, to stand" (Eph. 6:10–13).

PERSONAL ACTIVITIES

Reflect on times when you saw an opportunity to serve God or others but chose not to do so. What prevented you from jumping in? What was the outcome? What did you learn from that experience?

Make a list of opportunities for service that you are presently aware of at church, at work, or in your neighborhood. Then spend time in the coming week in prayer over each of these opportunities, asking the Lord to show you if He wants you to get involved—and if so, how.

MENTORING ACTIVITIES

Both partners should do the two personal activities above. Spend time together reviewing your lists of potential opportunities, and pray together over them. Select one opportunity from each list, and make a game plan together on how you will get involved—together, if possible.

> *"The supreme quality for leadership is unquestionable integrity. Without it, no real success is possible."*
>
> **—President Dwight Eisenhower** [1]

MAKING A PLAN

Noah lived in a time when the human race was at its very worst. Every thought and every plan of every person on earth was to devise evil. Things were so bad that God reached the point where He was actually sorry that He had made mankind (Gen. 6:6). That's bad!

It was because of this that God determined to destroy the entire human race—and all the rest of His living creatures on earth as well. Mankind's love for evil had been like a deadly infection, and that infection had spread to all living creatures on earth. So God made a plan of His own, a plan to send a flood of water that would cover the entire planet, drowning everything on earth.

But there was one exception to this wickedness, for we are told that Noah found grace in God's eyes. We don't know anything about him prior to his appearance in Genesis 5. We don't know what he did for a living, or for that matter where he lived. We learn that he had a wife, though we never learn her name, as well as three sons with their unnamed wives. But we do know that he was a righteous man, evidently the one light shining in that worldwide darkness.

And we also learn that he was a man who knew how to carry out a plan over a long period of time. The plan was actually God's, but the "carrying out" part was up to Noah (although, as we'll see, God helped him at every step). God laid out His plan to Noah, explaining that He intended to inundate the world with a great flood, but He also planned to save Noah and his entire family. He told Noah exactly what to do, to build a boat and stock it with provisions and animals of every kind. He spelled out the exact dimensions for that boat, telling Noah precisely how to construct it and what materials to use.

But there were a number of things about this plan that presented serious difficulties for Noah. First of all, God had promised to do something that had never happened in the history of the world: to drown the entire planet under water. Some go beyond this and suggest that it had never even rained on earth prior to Noah (based on Genesis 2:5–6), but that is not an important point. What matters is that God was asking Noah to prepare himself for a flood unlike anything ever seen on earth before that time (or since, for that matter), to believe in something that seemed utterly impossible simply because He said it would happen.

And those preparations were not an easy task. God told Noah what materials to use in building the ark, but He didn't tell him how or where to *get* them. He told him to secure enough food for himself, his family, and all those animals—some "of all food that is eaten" (Gen. 6:21)—but not how much or where to get it. Now, for all we know, Noah might have been a very wealthy man, but nobody could easily afford to buy enough lumber and materials to build a huge boat from scratch (it was about 450 feet long, the size of a World War I battleship), never mind enough food for hundreds of animals of every species plus eight people!

Then there was the matter of actually building the boat. Did Noah even know how to construct boats? Did he even know how to use a hammer and saw? And what about the reactions of people around him? We don't know these details for certain, but Peter tells us that Noah was "a preacher of righteousness" (2 Peter 2:5), so it is reasonable to assume that his neighbors—and family—asked him why he was building a huge ship in the middle of dry land. It seems quite likely that he was probably mocked and ridiculed by the world around him for believing God's Word about a coming flood.

But the first important thing to understand is that God miraculously provided the things Noah needed. We don't know how he secured the materials and food, but consider the difficult task that he was called to in gathering animals of every species on earth. Wild animals don't just follow you around when you call them, and simply finding two (or more) of every species on earth, from mice to elephants and sparrows to eagles, must have seemed like an impossible command to fulfill. The Bible does not tell us how he accomplished this—merely that he did. I tend to think that God somehow caused the animals to come to him, as He did for Adam during the week of creation (Gen. 2:19), but the important point is found in Genesis 7:5: "And Noah did according to all that the LORD commanded him."

The second important thing to take from Noah's life is that he had a plan. It was God's plan actually, since Noah would not have known about the coming flood if God had not revealed it to him. And the same principle holds true in our lives: God has a plan for what He wants each of us to do with our lifetimes, and He will reveal that to us when we have an attitude of obedience and willingness. But just as Noah needed to do some work to make that plan a reality, so we also need to do some work in understanding and implementing God's plan for our lives.

Noah carried out God's plan, obedient in all its details, despite the fact that it was very difficult—and despite the fact that it took an absolute minimum of twenty years to build it![2] There are two points here that are important: Noah's obedience and God's plan. In a similar way, I would suggest that there are two very important facets to finishing well and strong: obedience to God's commands, which we've been considering throughout this book, and having a plan.

Making a plan for finishing well and strong is what this chapter is about. We live in difficult days—although things today are probably not as bad as they were when Noah lived. Nevertheless, we know from Scripture that things are going to get worse in this world before it's over, and the need for planning is as urgent today as it was when Noah built the ark.

HOW TO MAKE A PLAN

The most important step in beginning a plan is to know where it ends. It's the same as any other journey; you can't very well plan out your route and supplies until you know where you're going. But knowing where you're going is only the beginning of the process. A trip to Antarctica could be a daunting thing to envision because it's so far away and hard to get to, but it would not be unattainable. You would plan such a trip by first deciding where you're going, then breaking it down into achievable steps.

That's what we need to do when we make a plan for our lives. We begin by determining where we want to be when we're done and work our way back from that. Let's walk through the steps.

LIFETIME GOAL

We'll take it for granted that you want to finish well and strong, since that's what this book is all about, but it's still a rather vague goal. You'll need to be more specific in determining what it means to finish well and strong, what you want that to look like in your own life. Noah's life goal was to be a righteous man who obeyed God's will, that much is clear—because you don't attain those goals without being deliberate about it; it doesn't happen by accident. But he also ended up being a sort of new Adam, the father of the entire human race. That would probably be an unrealistic goal for most of us today, and our life goals need to be something that we can both attain and measure.

Start by finishing this sentence: "I want to finish well and strong as a . . .": "I want to finish well and strong as a businessman whose workers see me as a role model," "as a craftsman whose work exemplifies my best efforts," "as a preacher of God's Word," "as a godly grandfather who is a loving example to his family," or "as a missionary overseas." This goal needs to be fairly specific, something that can be measured. You won't attain the goal of being a godly grandfather, for example, if you don't first marry and raise children. A man cannot become a missionary overseas if he doesn't first take steps to *go* overseas.

My lifetime goal is to be involved in discipling and evangelizing in the places where God sends me, including my recent work in the South Pacific, specifically in my adopted country of New Zealand. I want to utilize the specific gifts, talents, and experiences that God has given me in order to make me a unique member of His body, writing and speaking publicly to spread His Word.

FIVE-YEAR PLAN

The next step is to take your lifetime goal and try to picture where you'll need to be five years from now in your progress toward that final goal of finishing well and strong. Remember that finishing well and strong does not happen overnight; it's a long-term process. Noah did not build the ark overnight, or even in one year—he spent many years on the project, and probably grew tired and discouraged along the way. But he persevered.

Let's say that one of your lifetime goals is to become not only a successful businessman but one who has left a legacy of great integrity, honor, and products that make major contributions to mankind. You would need to prepare yourself to disciple younger executives in the methodology and approach to business that has made you successful. You would also need to be sure that your daily attitudes and character model a Christlike workplace.

My personal five-year plan incorporates opportunities to share the love of our Lord and His methodology with younger men preparing for ministry or who are now leading men's groups. I desire to spend more time with my wife and family members, helping them to know God more fully while making Him known.

ONE-YEAR PLAN

In order to fulfill your five-year plan, where will you need to be at the end of the first year? The first year is the time when you lay the groundwork and get things arranged for carrying out the five-year plan. Noah's first year was probably spent gathering materials, planting crops, making arrangements with people to provide things that he couldn't get himself, and so forth. Perhaps he needed tools that he didn't have; he most likely didn't have enough tar sitting around to completely seal a 450-foot boat!

The man who wants to establish a business with Christian core values starts by modeling a Christlike faith as he interacts with his employees. Next, he creates a team whose members share his values and vision and are willing to establish legacy projects with measurable goals. At the end of six months or a year, the employees and management evaluate their progress.

My own one-year plan includes making myself and ministry more available to Christian colleges and churches who want to influence their institutions with a deeper level of understanding about discipleship and ministry to men. Seeing the need and receptivity for evangelism in places like New Zealand, I want to lay a groundwork of relationships with missionaries and pastors there. My plans and goals for the future were not made in a vacuum, however; my wife, Louise, has been faithfully helping me shape these goals for our entire married life. Therefore, another of my one-year goals is to invest heavily into my beloved wife, helping her meet some of her own personal goals for the coming year.

ONE-MONTH PLAN

Now that we have the longer-range goals established, we're ready to become much more practical, figuring out the day-to-day tasks that are required to accomplish our one-year goal. This is where things become very doable, the sort of tasks that you feel confident you can accomplish within the coming month.

Noah, for example, might have determined that he needed to lay in a large quantity of tar for sealing the ark. So his one-month plan might have included "find a big tar pit—really big—and start collecting." This might have made him realize that he needed a place to store the tar, so he'd add, "Dig a pit with stone on the bottom." The man who wants to go on a mission to someplace like New Zealand must first start by looking at his calendar, speaking with his wife, and then establishing travel arrangements.

My own plan for the coming month is to finish this book—it's due to Thomas Nelson at the end of this month—and to take some R & R time with Louise. As it happens, we'll be going to New Zealand (see my one-year plan), but that trip will include some "Louise time" that I've already planned in. This accomplishes several things simultaneously: I'm working on my one-year plan by traveling to New Zealand; I'm working on Louise's plan (which is also part of my plan); and I'm rewarding us both with some overdue rest and relaxation.

DAILY TO-DO LISTS

This is the nitty-gritty, rubber-meets-the-road part of the lifetime goals. You've figured out what you need to accomplish in the coming year and have broken that down to what needs to happen in the coming month—now it's time to figure out what you will do tomorrow.

The previous steps were mostly goals, but this is a practical "I *will* do this tomorrow" list.

Noah might have written "make two pails" on his list of things to do tomorrow. If he knew that he'd have the whole day free, he might have added, "Design a rig for the mule to carry two pails of tar." The person wishing to do some ministry in New Zealand needs to put "Google 'Ministry opportunities in New Zealand'" and "Make a spreadsheet of traditions, challenges, opportunities, requirements, cost, etc." on his to-do list.

I've heard it said that it takes two weeks to make a habit, and two weeks to break one. As you make daily to-do lists to accomplish your one-month plan, you will be creating a new habit. By the time you have reached your one-month goal, you will have learned how to make and keep daily to-do lists, and you will have created a new habit of assessing and pursuing your lifetime goals.

My to-do list for today is to finish this chapter. That's it! This book is a top priority for me, and as the deadline approaches, I need to devote my entire time and attention to finishing it—and finishing it well. One important thing about to-do lists is to make sure that you can reasonably accomplish the task on the appointed day. There will always be surprises and curve balls, and sometimes you won't get something done, but the goal is to have more check marks for completed tasks than X-marks for things that didn't get done.

AT EVERY STEP

There are certain things that we will need to do at every step along the way in this process of setting and fulfilling life goals. These are general principles that will apply daily as we run the race toward finishing well and strong.

EXPECT SETBACKS AND OPPOSITION

We aren't told how Noah's family and neighbors reacted to his project of building a battleship in his yard, but I don't think it's a stretch to suggest that he probably faced some opposition and ridicule. His own family might have resisted the idea; it's even possible that some neighbors might have tried to prevent him in some way. We don't know the details, but we do know what's important: he finished well.

This does not mean that you disregard wise counsel as you make and execute your life's plans. Solomon warned repeatedly in Proverbs that a man needs to seek counsel if he wants his plans to succeed (e.g., Prov. 20:18). But any time we set out to obey God's leading in our lives, the enemy of our souls will attempt to discourage us and prevent us. You should expect such opposition before you even begin.

DON'T BE DISCOURAGED

Don't get discouraged when you miss a goal. And notice that I said *when*, not *if*. As I mentioned above, life will throw you curve balls and bring surprises, and there will be times when you fail to complete your daily to-do list. You might even find, at the end of the first year, that you didn't quite accomplish the goal you had set.

Noah undoubtedly suffered setbacks and discouragement, and perhaps even persecution from others, as he went about building the ark. But God was in complete control of all those events, and He used them to redirect Noah's efforts along the way. How do I know this? Because Noah *finished* the ark—and he finished well and strong.

God is in control of everything that comes into your life, and that includes the setbacks and surprises. Do not grow discouraged when you miss a goal. Remind yourself that God has it under control; be thankful and encouraged by whatever progress you have made; and press on!

TELL SOMEONE ELSE

Accountability is an absolute essential in accomplishing any plan, just as it is essential in the whole mentoring process. You need to be sure to tell someone else about your goals, preferably your mentoring partner and your spouse, people who can and will hold you accountable to attaining that goal.

You should also tell that person when you *accomplish* any goal. This does not need to include your daily to-do lists, although even that might be good to share with your wife. But certainly your mentoring partner needs to know when you attain your monthly goals, as that is part of the accountability relationship.

SET REWARDS

The ultimate reward for finishing well and strong will come from the Father when He says to you, "Well done, good and faithful servant!" But it's also helpful to have small rewards along the way to help you remember that you are working toward an eternal reward. The key word here is *small*; these are not intended to become a form of self-indulgence. That would be counterproductive, like a man who rewards himself for losing weight by eating a whole chocolate cake.

Try to include other people in your reward, such as having a movie night with the family when you complete a month's goal, or taking your mentoring partner to dinner. These sorts of rewards give you something to look forward to, while also helping to strengthen your godly relationships—which will, in turn, help you accomplish your goals.

DO IT WELL

The goal in this planning process is not simply to finish, but to finish *well and strong.* As I mentioned above, my plan for this month is to finish this book and get it to the publisher, but I am determined to do more than simply get it done—I want it to be a good book that furthers the kingdom of God.

The purpose of making plans is to know where we're going and figure out a way of getting there. But the purpose of our lives is to serve the Master, and that service needs to be done with excellence. At every step along your plan, remember that you want to do each task to the utmost of your ability. As Solomon wrote, "Whatever your hand finds to do, do it with your might" (Eccl. 9:10).

PERSONAL ACTIVITIES

Set aside one month of personal devotional times to establish and begin the process of planning to finish well and strong. This is an important undertaking, and it should not be rushed. Spend one week on each of the following steps. (This process works best when it is undertaken together with your mentoring partner, although this is not mandatory. See "Mentoring Activities" below.)

Week 1: Spend time in prayer and Bible study during the first week, asking God to help you visualize what it will mean in your life to finish well and strong. Ask Him to help you understand how He has been deliberately shaping who you are through your life's experiences, skills, spiritual gifts, and so forth. Ask Him to help you see what possible areas of service He has been deliberately shaping to fit you uniquely. Take notes as you go, and write down your life goal at the end of the week, being as specific as possible.

Week 2: Prayerfully reflect on where you will need to be in five years in order to be working toward your life goal. Again, be as specific as possible, and take notes as you go. Break that down into steps that will need to be accomplished along the way if it is to become a reality.

Week 3: Prayerfully put together a one-year plan. Use the notes from the previous week and your five-year plan. What steps are required along the way in accomplishing your five-year plan? What needs to be done in the first year of that process? What will you need to do in the coming months to accomplish what needs to be done by the end of the first year? At the end of this week, you should have a clear idea of what you need to accomplish in this coming year.

Week 4: Pray daily over your plans, asking God to help you fine-tune them and better understand how to accomplish them. Put together daily to-do lists, and ask Him to help you establish a habit of carrying out the tasks on those lists.

MENTORING ACTIVITIES

Both mentoring partners should undertake the "Personal Activities" above. Work together for the coming month on completing that activity, then hold each other accountable each week for the next month as you work on building a habit of pursuing your goals to finish well and strong.

Spend time together studying these verses from Proverbs: 15:22; 16:9; 19:21; 20:18; 21:5. What do you learn about planning from these proverbs? What part does your effort play in the process? What part does God play? What pitfalls should you avoid? What can you do to further your plans?

"Leaders aren't born, they are made. They are made by hard effort, which is the price which all of us must pay to achieve any goal which is worthwhile."

—Coach Vince Lombardi[1]

CROSSING THE FINISH LINE

I've had the privilege of being involved with six Ironman competitions. Now, before you get too excited, my involvement consisted of being the chaplain for the medical tent. My job description was to assist the doctors and nurses with distraught competitors who were having medical or emotional complications, either because they had to drop out or because they pushed themselves too hard to finish. Those who finished were needing help to try to process the emotions of pain and joy all at the same time.

The Ironman competition started in the late 1970s in Hawaii. Today, more than thirty-one qualifying events are held around the world so that the top participants can compete in the ultimate Ironman event on Kona, Hawaii. At this event, the best participants from various age groups will compete for the title as the best Ironman in the world.

It is interesting to watch the people as they pass the various mile markers associated with the features of this special marathon. Imagine swimming 2.4 miles, biking 112 miles, then finishing up the day with a run of 26.2 miles. Did I tell you that this all has to be done in seventeen hours or you will be disqualified? For most of us, driving in our comfortable air-conditioned car a total of 140.6 miles would be enough for one day.

The best time ever was posted on July 3, 2011, by Marino Vanhoenacker of Belgium at 7:45:58.[2]

The athletes who compete in the Ironman competitions are a special breed. They are committed and willing to sacrifice for the love of the challenge. It is especially interesting to see the athletes in the final five miles. They see the final markers along the way and seem to put a little kick into their run as each of the last mile markers appears. They become aware that the race is about to end and they desire to finish as strong as they were when they first started the day with the exhausting swim.

The Ironman competition resembles life. The swimming is kind of like those growing-up years. The bike race is like those precious family years, when building a family and career are foundational to the final years. And the running is similar to those last years of our lives, the so-called glory years, when our focus is on what we can do to leave our mark.

FINISHING STRONG

Recently, I attended a Sunday service where a senior pastor was retiring from full-time duty. This saint of the Lord was still going to be active in the life of the church but, after twenty-eight years, he chose to step down from being a full-time pastor. Pastor Al Hulten left all of us with a wonderful message that still lingers in my heart. Many of his thoughts about finishing well helped shape this chapter.

His thoughts reminded me of something Blaise Pascal wrote in his *Pensées* (literally "thoughts"): "The sole cause of man's unhappiness is that he does not know how to stay quietly in his room. . . . What people want is not the easy peaceful life that allows us to think of our unhappy condition, nor the dangers of war; not the burdens of office, but the agitation that takes our minds off it and diverts us. That is why we prefer the hunt to the capture. That is why men are so fond of hustle and bustle; that is why prison is such a fearful punishment; that is why the pleasures of solitude are so incomprehensible."[3] As I thought about Pastor Al's life, I couldn't help but ponder the importance of finishing well and strong like the marathon participants of the Ironman competitions. Pastor Al was a great role model for all of us to follow. He wasn't by nature a slow-poke, yet he never did things in a hurry just the same. He would take whatever time was needed to help people, counseling them in their troubles, offering sage advice, even helping with chores or financial emergencies. He has lived a full life, yet as he approaches the finish line, he isn't slowing down—if anything, he's speeding up! Like the Ironmen passing their final mile markers, Pastor Al is determined to pull out his last reserves of energy and pour it on strong at the end of his time here on earth. He's determined to finish as well as he started.

I've heard it said that life isn't a sprint but a marathon. As I'm past midlife and starting my journey down the backside of the mountain, I recognize the importance of our faith, family, and friends. How I finish life is more important to me than how I started. What people will most remember is whether I finish strong and remain focused on the end goal of glorifying God. And for those reading this book, continue to focus on the end goal. How we start is so important to setting a course to finish well. The apostle Paul said it best as he endeavored to encourage his disciple Timothy: "For I am already being poured out as a drink offering, and the time of my departure is at hand. I have fought the good fight, I have finished the race, I have kept the faith" (2 Tim. 4:6–7). He was encouraging Timothy to finish well, to imitate his example. And notice the metaphor Paul used: he compared his last years with a man who pours out a cup of wine as an offering to God. In other words, he intended to hold nothing back, but to pour out every last drop of energy and activity into the kingdom of God.

In His last days before going to the cross, Jesus prayed, "I have glorified You on the earth. I have finished the work which You have given Me to do. And now, O Father, glorify Me together with Yourself, with the glory which I had with You before the world was" (John 17:4–5). He had finished well and strong because He had obeyed what the Father had told Him to do—and in doing this, He had glorified the Father. In the same way, we glorify God when we finish well and strong, and we finish well and strong by obeying what He tells us to do, by pouring ourselves into His work like Paul.

THE WORLD VIEW VS. THE CHRISTIAN VIEW

In America, we measure success and significance, finishing well and finishing strong, by whether or not we have sufficient resources, financial security, enough nice material possessions, independence, a comfortable retirement, and a happy family life. Many place their value on having more than enough and a measureable amount of possessions.

It is interesting that Christ told us just the opposite. His idea of finishing well and strong (being successful) is found in the parable of the rich fool (Luke 12:13–21), which we discussed in a previous chapter. "Take heed and beware of covetousness," Jesus told His listeners, "for one's life does not consist in the abundance of the things he possesses" (v. 15). If we measure our success by what we have accumulated on earth, we are considered by God to be fools.

When the people I speak with about this subject are resistant to the message that Christ is giving us, I remind them that I've never conducted a funeral where there was a trailer attached to the hearse. But let me be clear on this matter. Many of the great wealthy Christians I know will be blessed and rewarded when they get to glory. I believe He is proud of His children when they are successful but willing to keep their focus on the one who made that possible. It is God who gives us the abilities to be successful.

Those people who have crossed my path, blessed our family and ministry, and contributed greatly to other eternal works have left a positive legacy for others to follow. They have embraced the Scripture that tells us, "For where your treasure is, there your heart will be also" (Luke 12:34). The evidence of their lives can be measured with more than material things.

The legacy we leave behind us is our mark on earth. We have left a fingerprint of our gifts, talents, personality, and the things we have done in this world. We all leave a mark. The issue is what kind of mark we will leave. There are many characters throughout history who have left a mark—but not one that would have any eternal significance. Powerful dictators who murdered thousands; notorious gangsters; even less-famous men and women who simply lived to indulge their desires—did their lives instill in others a sense of worth and purpose? Did their lives make positive changes in developing great character and a Christlike spirit in others?

Finishing well doesn't always mean that everyone is going to love us. Christ told His disciples, "Woe to you when all men speak well of you, for so did their fathers to the false prophets" (Luke 6:26). What was Christ telling us? I believe He wanted us to know that we won't always be loved or appreciated when we work to leave a positive mark on society. There will be those who love the things of darkness (sin) and they will detest anything of the Lord. Some will not like the brand of theology we are professing. Because of our brokenness and the brokenness of others, even as Christians we will find some people who are more difficult for us to love. Remember even God's perfect Son had many people who didn't love Him.

But Jesus was saying even more than this; He was actually saying that it's a *bad* sign when all the world speaks well of you! Having praise and adulation from the world around us is a signal that our priorities are not right, that they match the priorities of the world rather than those of God. That's why I keep repeating that we need to stand guard against the temptation of chasing after the world's ideas of success. When we do that, we are in danger of setting ourselves in opposition to God.

When I'm feeling down or discouraged because I'm not getting the appreciation of others, I go to Galatians 1:10: "For do I now persuade men, or God? Or do I seek to please men? For if I still pleased men, I would not be a bondservant of Christ." In other words, am I living to impress the world around me with my success and security— or am I living to please God with my obedience and service? Paul is telling us, once again, that those two goals are mutually exclusive; we simply cannot please the world and please God at the same time.

There are many religious leaders, professional athletes, and political figures who made some great contributions, but for whatever reason didn't finish well. They let the temptations of pride, greed, wealth, influence, lust, or power get in their way. Is there anything in your path that needs to be explored so you can be counted among those who finished well?

HOW CAN WE FINISH WELL?

I want to now focus on four things that will help us finish well and strong. God's Word will help guide our thinking on these concepts.

1. Be aware that temptation is around you. Despite our circumstances and difficulties to stay strong, there are many potential road hazards that can cause our journey to go off track. Sometimes we begin to believe that we have experienced the most challenging times in our younger years. The temptations of youth and lustful thoughts may have lessened in intensity, but we can still be led astray and fall into sinful behavior, no matter what our age.

Stay the course and remember that none of us is exempt from the temptations of the world. The author of Hebrews urges us:

> Therefore we also, since we are surrounded by so great a cloud of witnesses, let us lay aside every weight, and the sin which so easily ensnares us, and let us run with endurance the race that is set before us, looking unto Jesus, the author and finisher of our faith, who for the joy that was set before Him endured the cross, despising the shame, and has sat down at the right hand of the throne of God. (Heb. 12:1–2)

There are numerous elements to note in these verses. First, we must run our race with endurance—and endurance means pouring on whatever reserves we have at the end of the race, like the Ironman competitors during the marathon stage. Our temptation is to do the opposite, to tell ourselves as we get older, "I've worked hard to earn what I have, and now it's time to enjoy it." And when we say that, we are talking like the rich fool in Jesus' parable, not like a man who finishes well and strong.

Notice also that the writer of Hebrews implied that sin "so easily ensnares us" at any age. Getting older does not mean that temptations become less strong or dangerous; it only means that the temptations are toward different sins. All sin is deadly, and if anything, sin at the end of the race can be more devastating than earlier on, because there is less time left to make corrections.

Hebrews also tells us that we are surrounded by a "cloud of witnesses." That means that our lives are being watched, that God and His servants are paying attention to how we finish our race. This is a sobering thought, because it's easy to think to ourselves, *Nobody is going to know.* This is false thinking, and it can lead us into serious error. But the flip side of this is very encouraging: we have a host of cheerleaders rooting for our success! God *wants* us to finish well and strong, and He fully intends to help us in that endeavor.

And this leads us to the final thing I want to mention regarding this passage: we do these things by "looking unto Jesus." I've said many times in this book that we learn best by imitating a good example, and Jesus is the ultimate example of what it means to finish well and strong. He is "the author and finisher of our faith," which means that He fully intends to finish what He started, He fully intends to help us finish well. For Him, that meant enduring the cross and despising its shame, but in the end He sat down at the right hand of God. We need to expect that finishing well will involve some degree of suffering or hardship as well, but in the end we, too, will sit with Jesus before the Father—if we endure to the end and always remind ourselves of the joy that is waiting for us.

Some very prominent Christian leaders have fallen and more will fall because often Satan tempts us to think we are secure. If we think that being tempted with lustful thoughts isn't possible—guess what? That new secretary in your office whose heart was just broken by her boyfriend may find your secure and comforting manner just the thing to satisfy her desires. When you believe that the love of money isn't a temptation—guess what? Someone will offer you a chance to double your investment by simply giving them part of your retirement funds. We all have those moments of weakness when we need to be reminded of the possibility that we could be the target for one of Satan's darts. As Paul reminds us, "Therefore let him who thinks he stands take heed lest he fall. No temptation has overtaken you except such as is common to man; but God is faithful, who will not allow you to be tempted beyond what you are able, but with the temptation will also make the way of escape, that you may be able to bear it" (1 Cor. 10: 12–13). When you find yourself tempted to sin, you need to remember that your temptation is not something new and unique; it's common to all men. And those temptations are all the more likely to sneak up on us when we're thinking that we've gotten past the point of *being* tempted. But God is faithful, and He will always provide the way out of that temptation. Our job, then, is to stand firm in resisting it all the way to the end of the race.

2. Have a strong and vibrant spiritual life. It is through a fervent prayer life, meditating on God's Word, living in obedience to His calling, and developing a relationship with a spiritual mentor that we can remain strong. God commanded Joshua, "This Book of the Law shall not depart from your mouth, but you shall meditate in it day and night, that you may observe to do according to all that is written in it. For then you will make your way prosperous, and then you will have good success" (Josh. 1:8). How do we make ourselves successful? By meditating daily on God's Word, and by deliberately and carefully ensuring that we obey it. And one way of helping with that process is to talk about God's Word with others, by sprinkling it into every conversation. This is what God meant when He commanded Joshua not to let His Word "depart from your mouth."

To sprint to the finish line with the wind (Holy Spirit) behind our back is the final goal for the Christian. God created us for relationship—first with Him and then with others. He desires an intimate relationship that is built on trust, obedience, love, and faithfulness.

Jesus told His listeners that the greatest commandment is to "love the Lord your God with all your heart, with all your soul, with all your mind, and with all your strength." And the second commandment, He said, is just like it: "You shall love your neighbor as yourself" (Mark 12:29–31). So the two greatest commandments of all are both concerned with our relationships: our relationship with God, and our relationships with everyone around us.

3. Complete the work God wants you to do. What has God placed upon your heart? If you now have a little time, some resources, and a desire to make a real difference, what are some things that God has put before you that resonate with your interest, gifts, and talents? The apostle Paul had that opportunity. "But none of these things move me," he told his audience, speaking of the things that he had suffered for the sake of the gospel, "nor do I count my life dear to myself, so that I may finish my race with joy, and the ministry which I received from the Lord Jesus, to testify to the gospel of the grace of God" (Acts 20:24). He was not concerned with his previous sufferings, and he

CROSSING THE FINISH LINE

was not concerned with losing his present freedom—he was only concerned with spreading the gospel of Jesus Christ.

The Ironmen I know don't try to look five miles down the road to the next marker. No, they look about ten yards in front of them while they are telling themselves, "Just ten more yards." Our Lord wants us to have God-sized dreams and to tackle those dreams one day at a time. If we look at the enormous tasks before us, we can become overwhelmed and give up. Line up and conquer the daily short-term goals so that at the end of a year or five years you have indeed tackled the God-sized vision.

A word of caution: We need to balance our priorities and recognize that there will always be the needy around us. I have great difficulty saying no to some very good opportunities to serve. I constantly need to take the time to evaluate my strengths, abilities, interests, and talents in light of the end goals I've established. Don't take on a task just because you can. Learn to place the items before God in prayer, ask the Holy Spirit to teach and guide you, and properly evaluate those opportunities through the lens of Scripture and godly counsel. Select the best things to focus upon. The good to fair things may be better for someone else to take.

4. Know that starting well doesn't mean you finish well. Scripture provides two great examples of men who processed life differently as related to finishing well. On Paul's first missionary journey, Barnabas asked if his cousin John Mark could join them (Col. 4:10). The men began their preaching and teaching of the good news in Barnabas's hometown of Cyprus (Acts 13:4–5). After some success, they proceeded to Perga, where John Mark left them to return to Jerusalem.

We aren't sure why he returned home. Whatever the reason for his leaving, it greatly upset Paul because he clearly viewed Mark's departure as desertion. Mark was one of those whose commitment faltered, and Paul was hardened against him.

As Paul and Barnabas planned their second missionary journey, Barnabas wanted to give the young John Mark another chance, but Paul refused to permit him to come along. (Barnabas lived up to the meaning of his name as a "son of consolation" or "encouragement.") The dispute between Paul and Barnabas grew so heated that the two parted, and Paul took Silas on the second journey, while Barnabas took Mark and went to Cyprus.

The Christians in Judea and surrounding areas were suffering much. There was a famine, persecution of Christians, the stoning of Stephen, and the imprisonment of Peter (Acts 7–8; 12). When others were leaving the Christ-followers, John Mark seems to have rekindled his efforts and became a vibrant follower. He even sheltered and comforted the disciples in his home. Paul and Barnabas thought so much of John Mark's commitment that they asked him to rejoin them (2 Tim. 4:11; 1 Peter 5:13).

John Mark became consumed with Christ and was the writer of the gospel of Mark and a scribe for Peter. Mark's gospel is directed to the Gentiles and Romans of his day. He explains Jewish customs and seems to have a special interest in the persecution and martyrdom of believers. By all accounts, John Mark finished well and left a legacy of great faith to all who read his writings.

On the other end of the spectrum was a guy named Demas. He was a companion of the apostle Paul during his first imprisonment at Rome, and Paul referred to him as his fellow worker (Philem. 24; Col. 4:14). Imagine sitting chained up to Paul in a cold Roman prison while he was winning the guards over to Christianity with his bold testimony. Demas had a front-row seat to see Paul the evangelist in action. Undoubtedly he read the letters that Paul wrote from prison about finishing well. And yet Paul wrote this sad commentary about Demas: "Demas has forsaken me, having loved this present world, and has departed for Thessalonica" (2 Tim. 4:10). Demas was lured away from finishing well because his focus was on the things of the world. If we are to finish well, we need the Lord to stand by us and strengthen us, that the message of our Lord might be preached. And like Paul and Mark, we will be counted among the faithful.

Paul recognized that he was at the end of his life—he was spent (2 Tim. 4). He reminded the younger Timothy to hang in there. "Preach the word! Be ready in season and out of season. Convince, rebuke, exhort, with all longsuffering and teaching. For the time will come when they will not endure sound doctrine, but according to their own desires, because they have itching ears, they will heap up for themselves teachers; and they will turn their ears away from the truth, and be turned aside to fables. But you be watchful in all things, endure afflictions, do the work of an evangelist, fulfill your ministry" (2 Tim. 4:2–5). These were Paul's final remarks to Timothy prior to his execution in Rome. In these remarks, Paul lists four important tasks of the man who finishes well and strong.

Be watchful in all things. As I've already said, temptation and sin are not restricted to young men. Even as we get older, we need to be constantly alert to the ways the world around us tries to seduce us away from obedience to God's Word. Paul doesn't say "be watchful against sexual temptation," but be alert in *all things.* This suggests that a man can be prevented from finishing well by many areas of sin and failure. That list actually does not get shorter as we get older; it merely gets longer. The man who finishes well and strong will keep himself alert at all times, with his eyes always focused on the goal of eternal reward.

Endure afflictions. As I've been saying throughout this book, following Christ brings a guarantee of some suffering and hardship. We should not become discouraged by expecting the Christian life to be nothing but sadness and self-sacrifice, but we also need to recognize that there will be some sadness and sacrifice along the way. Paul counseled Timothy that he needed to be willing to persevere, to endure that hardship as part of the cost of finishing well. The Ironman competitors endured much physical discomfort as they competed, but they were willing to do so because they longed to cross the finish line. We need to cultivate that same attitude.

Do the work of an evangelist. Not everyone is called to be an evangelist like Billy Graham. That is a specific gift that only some people are given (Eph. 4:11). All the same, every Christian is called to do the work of an evangelist, because every Christian is called to be a living model of Jesus Christ. Remember that people are watching you, and some are even imitating you! When we live a godly life and strive to finish well, we are doing the work of an evangelist.

Fulfill your ministry. What ministry has God called you to? For one thing, as I've already said, He has called you to do the work of an evangelist by living in obedience to His Word. But if you are a father, then He has also called you to the ministry of raising God-fearing children. If you are a businessman, then part of your ministry is to model Christ at work. And ultimately, part of your ministry is to finish well and strong, which is what this whole book is about.

PERSONAL ACTIVITIES

Take four sheets of paper and write the following headings on them: watchful in all things; enduring afflictions; doing the work of an evangelist; fulfilling my ministry. Then make a list of specific things in your life that fit into each category. Which category needs to be strengthened? How can you find encouragement to persevere in the face of affliction? How strong is your testimony for Christ? What areas of ministry need some attention?

MENTORING ACTIVITIES

Both partners should do the personal exercise above. Spend time together reviewing your lists, helping each other find things you missed and expand on things included. Then hold each other accountable in the coming month to fulfill your ministries and strengthen your testimonies in your daily lives.

"If you judge people, you have no time to love them."
—**Mother Teresa**[1]

THE FINISH LINE

We began this book with the question "What does it mean to finish well and strong?" We've considered many illustrations and analogies along the way to help us understand this concept, but the one we'll conclude with is the picture of a marathon runner.

How a runner begins the race can make a difference, in that he needs to pace himself and run strong and consistently throughout the race. But at the end of the race, there is only one thing that really matters: crossing the finish line going strong. I've interviewed a number of professional marathon athletes after their races, and they tell me that to finish well and strong they want nothing in reserve left at the end—that they have no regrets about holding back.

A runner might stumble along the route; he might grow weary and lose position as he goes; he might even have made a large tactical error at the beginning when the gun went off. These things happen all the time to world-class athletes, and yet they still manage to set records and take home gold medals. Again, I think back on Billy Mills's victory and how he came from behind to win his race.

When committed athletes make a mistake, they don't sit down on the sidelines and weep or give up; they keep going and work to make up for lost time. They win, not because they run flawlessly but because they keep their eyes on the finish line at all times.

Let's review some of the major principles we've considered throughout this book and try to summarize some of what it means to finish well and strong.

FINISHING WELL MEANS LIVING LIKE CHRIST

This is where our marathon analogy breaks down. Finishing well looks different to everyone in the race. For an elite marathon runner it means winning. For some it means doing better than they did in their last marathon. For others it just means being able to run through the finish line, no matter the time or placing. But to the Christian finishing well in our lives means only one thing: doing what we can to resemble Jesus, regardless of what other people do.

As mature believers we should not measure our success by comparing ourselves with others; we measure it by comparing ourselves to Christ. It also means that, for the Christian, most often finishing well is about having a team surrounding you, fellow believers who are encouragers, mentors, and team members who have the same vision and heart to honor our Lord.

> A disciple is not above his teacher, nor a servant above his master. It is enough for a disciple that he be like his teacher, and a servant like his master. (Matt. 10:24–25)

WHERE YOUR TREASURE IS, THERE YOUR HEART WILL BE

You can easily tell where your treasure lies by paying attention to what things are your top priorities. We need to reassess our treasure on a regular basis, frequently readjusting our priorities on time, money, and energies. The things we gather in this life—reputation, wealth, success—will all pass away. Jesus said that earthly gains are like wood, hay, and stubble, and they will all be burned to ashes; but eternal pursuits are fireproof, bringing rewards that last forever.

Can you be financially successful and still be focused upon kingdom issues? Sure you can. Many very successful people have properly balanced and allocated their time and treasure to live a life that fully glorifies our Lord. It becomes harder to keep one's focus on heavenly treasure as we increase worldly distractions and pursuits, but make no mistake that those fortunate wealthy people who can properly focus their hearts on Christ and His kingdom can make a major impact upon ministries and important things influencing the lives of many.

> For where your treasure is, there your heart will be also. (Matt. 6:21)

REMEMBER THAT YOUR DAYS ARE NUMBERED

In an earlier chapter, we considered the difference between the world's philosophy by considering two Latin phrases: *carpe diem*, seize the day; and *memento mori*, remember that you will die. Rather than trying to seize the day to gain success, wealth, power, or prestige, we must seize every opportunity to lay up treasure in eternity. No man has an unlimited supply of time; every one of us must one day die. Involve yourself and set your priorities for things that impact God's kingdom.

We discussed the importance of the dash between the date you were born and the date you go to be with Jesus. The dash represents what you did during that time. How are you using your time on earth to know God and make Him known? What contributions are you making that have eternal value for you and others?

> For what profit is it to a man if he gains the whole world, and loses his own soul? Or what will a man give in exchange for his soul? (Matt. 16:26)

DEVELOP A ZEAL FOR GOD'S KINGDOM

This principle is the corollary to the last one, sort of the opposite side to the same coin. Remembering that our days are numbered is only half the equation; we must also live out those days deliberately rather than passively. If your treasure is being stored up in heaven, then it only makes sense to build that treasure with enthusiasm and all your strength, to pursue the kingdom of God with zeal. Remember Solomon's advice: "Whatever your hand finds to do, do it with your might; for there is no work or device or knowledge or wisdom in the grave where you are going" (Eccl. 9:10).

For many years, the concept of becoming self-sufficient or self-actualizing is how most of us have thought about life. Get all you can get! The notion of "it's about me and my stuff" has been promoted in the media and mainstream educational institutions. For many, sufficiency is now measured not just on survival but on how big your bank account is, how many televisions you own, how many cell phones you have in your home, and how we can impress others with all our stuff.

I suggest that Christ's life is a testimony of how we contribute to the world around us as we move through life. We need not wait until we "make it" before we assist others. Your involvement might be volunteering at a food bank or homeless shelter. Certainly our churches have plenty of need for those willing to provide resources and time to assist with their mission.

How would our lives and service to others look if we viewed life differently? The reality is we can't go two directions at the same time. Trying to place our primary focus on accumulating stuff while having an eternal perspective on life is like driving down the freeway at seventy miles per hour and constantly looking at your rearview mirror. Our primary focus needs to be on what God's plan is for our lives and how He can use us in the future. If we are in His plan, then we know that we will have the very best.

REMAIN TEACHABLE THROUGHOUT YOUR LIFE

A teachable spirit is vital for the man who wants to finish well and strong. We never reach a point in life where we have it all together, where we are exempt from temptation or sin. Nobody ever becomes perfect or entirely like Christ in this world, and that means that the Holy Spirit will continue teaching us and making us more like Christ as long as we live. But He cannot make those changes if we refuse to change. A man who refuses to change and learn becomes like dried-out clay that the potter can no longer mold, and such a man generally does not finish well.

We most often learn by listening, reading God's Word, meditating, and being directed by the Holy Spirit. To be a good leader (influencer), you need wisdom and guidance that goes beyond your education, experience, and network of contacts. You need the counsel of the Holy Spirit. One of the greatest joys I have is to listen to others, especially younger people, and hear what they are thinking. It simulates my creativity and vision and assists me in mentoring them.

The greatest gift and respect someone can give you is *time*. The gift of yourself to someone else is a valuable *gift*. If we remain teachable throughout our lives and seek to invest in others, we will find a source of renewal and strength that exceeds our expectations. It will also bring great joy to yourself and those being mentored.

> Be diligent to present yourself approved to God, a worker who does not need to be ashamed, rightly dividing the word of truth. (2 Tim. 2:15)

DO JUSTLY, LOVE MERCY, WALK HUMBLY WITH GOD

Micah 6:8 summarizes all that God wants from His children, the things that He considers good and which He requires from anyone who wants to finish well: "He has shown you, O man, what is good; and what does the LORD require of you but to do justly, to love mercy, and to walk humbly with your God?" Make this your life's verse, reminding yourself of it daily and taking a daily assessment of those three things: do justly; love mercy; walk humbly.

The men who have had the greatest influence on my life are those who have endeavored to walk humbly. They most often aren't the superstars in sports, politics, and entertainment that I've had the privilege to associate with, but are common Joes who walk their talk and model a Christlike life. They are the prayer warriors I go to when I need encouragement. They are the people who seek to know God and make Him known. I listen to the men who have been in the battles and have found ways to deal with pain and challenges—men who started with nothing and have used their success to give glory to God in their deeds, actions, and gifts. Pastor Al in chapter 14 is an example of the kind of people that are major influencers in my life.

> He has shown you, O man, what is good;
> And what does the LORD require of you
> But to do justly,
> To love mercy,
> And to walk humbly with your God? (Mic. 6:8)

SEEK FIRST THE KINGDOM OF GOD AND HIS RIGHTEOUSNESS

Jesus commanded His disciples, "Seek first the kingdom of God and His righteousness" (Matt. 6:33). Throughout this book we have considered what it means to seek the kingdom of God and His righteousness. This does not mean that we ignore other issues of life; part of seeking His kingdom is to be responsible for the welfare of others around us. Jesus said that we should seek His kingdom and righteousness *first*, which suggests that there are also other things in life that demand our time and attention. But our top priority should always be on loving God with all our heart, mind, and strength, and loving others as ourselves.

When we seek the kingdom of God, we gradually learn to place the interests of others above our own interest. Scripture tells us not to love ourselves but to love others *as* we love ourselves (Rom. 13:9). Your influence as a leader is often determined by how abundantly you place other people's interests first. And your value as a contributor is determined by how much more you give than what you receive.

> For the commandments, "You shall not commit adultery," "You shall not murder," "You shall not steal," "You shall not bear false witness," "You shall not covet," and if there is any other commandment, are all summed up in this saying, namely, "You shall love your neighbor as yourself." (Rom. 13:9)

DO NOT BE AFRAID

God commands His people repeatedly throughout Scripture, "Do not be afraid!" If He repeats it so frequently, it must be important. Remember Gideon, who was cowering in a wine vat because he was afraid of the powerful army that threatened to steal his crops. Remember David, who stood alone and barely armed against a powerful foe who towered above him. Read Hebrews 11 and meditate on the many men and women in the Bible who faced terrible odds in the name of God— and remember how God saved them and made them heroes, time and time again. Do not give in to fear, but trust in God's faithfulness.

Finishing well and strong often requires courage. We might think that by gaining enough experience or people skills we would not experience fear, become less timid and more bold—but then some circumstance beyond our control knocks that notion flat. And people who have caring hearts are apt to take on fears from the circumstances in the lives of others. When fear does grip our hearts, we need to remember what Moses told the people of Israel when they were about to be overrun by the Egyptian army:

> And Moses said to the people, "Do not be afraid. Stand still, and see the salvation of the LORD, which He will accomplish for you today. For the Egyptians whom you see today, you shall see again no more forever." (Ex. 14:13)

GOD SHAPES US FOR HIS SPECIFIC CALLING

Moses lived through a number of unusual experiences when he was growing up, experiences that made him unique. He didn't know it at the time, but God was shaping him specifically for the calling of leading His people out of Egypt and into the promised land. God has done the same with you—and not only that, but He is also preparing a specific calling that is shaped just to fit you. Look for ways to capitalize on what makes you unique as you seek His kingdom.

The experiences of our lives, as unpleasant as some might be, are shaping us for His glory and preparing us to assist others in their struggles. Trials can strengthen our faith, increase our devotion to Christ, and help purify and sanctify our lives. As gold or silver is refined through the purifying process involving heat and removal of unwanted materials, so it is with our lives. God wants to strengthen our faith, our reliance upon Him, while removing from us those impurities that create blemishes in our Christlike modeling.

> My brethren, count it all joy when you fall into various trials, knowing that the testing of your faith produces patience. But let patience have its perfect work, that you may be perfect and complete, lacking nothing. (James 1:2–4)

PERSONAL ACTIVITIES

Let me suggest some ideas you can prayerfully consider:

1. Pray that the Holy Spirit will direct your paths.

2. Consult with a godly mentor, pastor, or friend.

3. Involve your family in your decision-making process.

4. Develop short-term and long-term goals.

5. With the power of the Holy Spirit conquer your fears and overcome your doubt; move forward.

6. Inventory your skills, abilities, talents, gifts, experience, and education.

7. Focus on things with eternal consequences.

8. Be intentional about growing in your faith.

9. Work with a life coach to assist you in a life plan.

   a. Develop a vision statement (personal, family, and business)
   b. Identify the things that drive your spiritual passions
   c. Consider the things that bring spiritual fulfillment
   d. Evaluate your key business principles and practices
   e. Develop a plan to apply your vision statements
   f. Have a method of operation on how your goals and objectives can be implemented
   g. Deliberately plan on *finishing well and finishing strong*.

MENTORING ACTIVITIES

Discuss with your mentor the nine items mentioned in the previous section. Be intentional about setting a timeline to work on the items. Identify the other resources needed to fulfill your vision statement and plan. Ask for specific prayer, guidance, and accountability on the items.

EPILOGUE

Finishing well and finishing strong doesn't mean that we won't grow weary along the way. Even our Lord recognized the importance of rest for His weary soul as He slept in front of the boat (Mark 4:37–38) and removed Himself from the crowds (Mark 6:31). Christ left the world with many people still to be healed, countless yet to know His ministry, and millions of broken individuals needing His saving grace. I don't think God expects you or me to meet every need of others. He wants His army of believers to join together and accomplish His mission. We are part of a big team of disciples.

Ministry to others is what God desires us to do throughout our lives, but we are to balance our lives with the things that make life abundant and joyful. This is something that I am still working on. We can and will grow weary serving others, but our Lord promises to uphold us during our weary times. The *power* of the Holy Spirit, the *grace* of a crucified Savior, and the *mercy* of a loving God will help sustain us through the most trying times.

Seek God's greatest blessings and treasures for your life. His Word tells us, "For where your treasure is, there your heart will be also" (Matt. 6:21). This is where you will find true joy and success. To paraphrase a theory I've heard, *there are three sources of unhappiness in life. One is not getting what you want, the second is getting it, and the third is not feeling that you have left anything of true significance to future generations.* Ponder the meaning of this in your life and experiences.

When you find God's treasure for your life, pass on those values, experiences, successes, and, yes, even lessons learned during your failures to future generations.

God bless you and your time in making an eternal difference. And, in the final analysis, as you strive to love God and others, to be obedient to the One who is the Savior and Lord of lords and King of kings, you can rest assured that He will greet you with, "Well done, good and faithful servant" (Matt. 25:21). What could ever be better than that?

ACKNOWLEDGMENTS

I praise God for the men in my life who have demonstrated to me how to *finish well and finish strong*. Not everyone leaves a mark of significance for future generations to emulate. Worldly success can be measured by fame, fortune, power, prestige, position, and possessions, but these criteria aren't necessarily connected with living a life that has significance. Jesus, the apostle Paul, the disciples, Saint Francis of Assisi, Mother Teresa, Dietrich Bonhoeffer, Martin Luther, John Wesley, Billy Graham, and others did not have the material accumulations that typically define a successful life, yet they all lived lives of great significance. The legacy and heritage they left for future generations still vibrate through changed lives and their written records.

I also wish to acknowledge my friends at Thomas Nelson and Gregory C. Benoit for their assistance in preparing this work. You are much appreciated.

I cannot begin to thank those men who inspired me with their lives and testimonies. Your modeling of a Christlike life has been a real encouragement to me. Certainly my wife, Louise, deserves another call-out for her patience and heart of support in sacrificing the time that was necessary from my family for me to complete yet another project.

When we think about people who really exemplify sacrifice and living a life of significance, we can't forget those who served in the military or as first responders. Thank you for all your efforts in showing us how to model a life of significance even unto death.

I especially wish to thank Career Press and Peggy Anderson for allowing me to utilize the quotes found at the beginning of some of the chapters. These are from their book *Great Quotes from Great Leaders*.

NOTES

DEDICATION

1. Goodreads. Accessed June 5, 2014. http://www.goodreads.com/quotes/232517-what-we-do-for-ourselves-dies-with-us-what-we.

INTRODUCTION

1. Charles Dickens, *A Tale of Two Cities* (Oxford: Oxford University Press, 1998), 1.
2. *Saving Private Ryan,* Dir. Steven Spielberg, Paramount Pictures, 1998. Quoted on IMDb, "Saving Private Ryan Quotes," accessed March 17, 2014. http://www.imdb.com/title/tt0120815/quotes.
3. Chuck Swindoll, *A Life Well Lived* (Nashville: Thomas Nelson, 2007), xiv. Used by permission. All rights reserved.

CHAPTER 1

1. Michael Lynberg, *Make Each Day Your Masterpiece: Practical Wisdom for Living an Exceptional Life* (Kansas City, MO: Andrew McMeel Publishing, 2001), 181.
2. Unless otherwise indicated, all dictionary definitions are from *The New Shorter Oxford English Dictionary,* Lesley Brown, ed. (Oxford: Clarendon Press, 1993).
3. Steve Farrar, *Finishing Strong* (Colorado Springs, CO: Multnomah Publishers, 1995), 19.
4. *The Journals of Jim Elliot,* ed. Elisabeth Elliot (NY: Fleming H. Revell, 1978), 174.

CHAPTER 2

1. *Great Quotes from Great Leaders,* compiled by Peggy Anderson (Naperville, IL: Simple Truths, 2007), 10.

CHAPTER 3

1. Wayne Hogue, *Elements of Leaders of Character* (Bloomington, IN: WestBow Press, 2013), 155.
2. David Blankenhorn, *Fatherless America: Confronting Our Most Urgent Social Problem* (New York: Basic Books, 1995), 1.

CHAPTER 4

1. Addie Johnson, *A Little Book of Thank Yous: Letters, Notes & Quotes* (San Francisco, CA: Red Wheel/Weiser, 2010), 11.

2. Chuck Stecker, *Men of Honor, Women of Virtue* (Denver, CO: Seismic Publishing Group, 2010), p. 196–197.
3. For this analogy, I am indebted to Richard J. Mouw, *Uncommon Decency* (Downers Grove, IL: InterVarsity Press, 2010), 149–50.
4. Author unknown, 1949, Thinkexist.com. Accessed June 6, 2014. http://thinkexist.com/quotation/excellence_can_be_obtained_if_you-care_more_than/9638.html.

CHAPTER 5

1. *Great Quotes from Great Leaders*, 13.
2. Lloyd Reeb, *Success to Significance* (Grand Rapids: Zondervan, 2004), 18.
3. Ibid, 14.

CHAPTER 6

1. *Great Quotes from Great Leaders*, 22.
2. All quotations from Jack Countryman are from an interview with the author, February 17, 2014.
3. Quoted by John C. Maxwell in *Leadership 101: What Every Leader Needs to Know* (Nashville: Thomas Nelson, 2002), 76.
4. Bob Buford, *Halftime* (Grand Rapids: Zondervan, 2008), 37.

CHAPTER 7

1. *Great Quotes from Great Leaders*, 54.
2. For more information on this topic, see *Muhammad Ali: His Life and Times* by Thomas Hauser (New York: Simon and Schuster, 1992).
3. Winston Churchill, "We Shall Fight on the Beaches," accessed Feb. 27, 2014. http://www.winstonchurchill.org/learn/speeches/speeches-of-winston-churchill/128-we-shall-fight-on-the-beaches.

CHAPTER 8

1. John R. Brokhoff, *Pray like Jesus: An Exploration in Prayer* (Lima, OH: The CSS Publishing Co., 1994), 56.
2. I am taking the liberty of adding extra details to the parable that Jesus actually taught, in order to help us understand it better. You can read His parable in Luke 12.
3. New World Encyclopedia, "John D. Rockefeller," https://www.newworld encyclopedia.org/entry/John_D._Rockefeller, accessed March 3, 2014.

CHAPTER 9

1. *Great Quotes from Great Leaders*, 96.
2. David Jeremiah, *What Are You Afraid Of?* (Carol Stream, IL: Tyndale House Publishers, 2013), 90.

3. Ibid.

CHAPTER 10

1. *Great Quotes from Great Leaders*, 89.
2. All the quotations regarding the Billy Mills story are taken from www
.kuathletics.com/news/2013/9/26/TRACK_0926133117.aspx. Accessed
January 30, 2014.
3. C. S. Lewis, *The Problem of Pain* (New York: The MacMillan Company,
1971), 93.

CHAPTER 11

1. *Great Quotes from Great Leaders*, 102.

CHAPTER 12

1. *Great Quotes from Great Leaders*, 91.
2. Don Davis, speech given at an Iron Sharpens Iron Conference in Rancho
Cordova, October 12, 2013.
3. Theodore Roosevelt, "The Strenuous Life," speech given before the
Hamilton Club, Chicago, April 10, 1899; from WikiQuote.org, accessed
March 13, 2014. https://en.wikiquote.org/wiki/Theodore_Roosevelt.

CHAPTER 13

1. http://thinkexist.com/quotation/the_supreme_quality_for_leadership_
is/202972.html.
2. Bodie Hodge, "How Long Did It Take for Noah to Build the Ark?"
Answers in Genesis, June 1, 2010, accessed March 8, 2014. http://www
.answersingenesis.org/articles/2010/06/01/long-to-build-the-ark.

CHAPTER 14

1. *Great Quotes from Great Leaders*, 53.
2. http://www.ironman.com/triathlon-news/articles/2011/07/
vanhoenacker-world-best-time-in-austria-and-slideshow.
aspx#axzz2t4eTKBSy, accessed February 12, 2014.
3. Blaise Pascall, *Pensees*, tr. A. J. Krailsheimer (New York: Penguin, 1995),
37.

CHAPTER 15

1. *Great Quotes from Great Leaders*, 25.

ABOUT THE AUTHOR

Dr. Jim Grassi is an award-winning author, communicator, outdoorsman, pastor, and former television cohost. He has presented hundreds of messages and programs around the world that helped equip people to fulfill the Great Commission (Matthew 28). He brings a sense of challenge, wisdom, excitement, and humor to his presentations, as he connects with people of various cultures and backgrounds. Through his multimedia outreach ministry, he encourages participants toward a greater understanding and appreciation of evangelism, discipleship, and the development of creating vibrant men's ministries.

Jim Grassi is the founder and president of the culturally strategic Men's Ministry Catalyst, an organization he incorporated in 1981. Grassi is also the author of several books, magazine articles, booklets, and tracts.

Dr. Grassi has appeared on many radio and television programs including *Hour of Power, The 700 Club, The Carol Lawrence Show,* Cornerstone Television, Southern Baptist Television—*Cope,* Chicago Television 38, *The Dick Staub Show, Getting Together, In-Fisherman, Fishing Tales, Jimmy Houston Outdoors, Home Life,* FOX Sports, and CSN.

Grassi was born and reared in the San Francisco Bay area. Known for his evangelistic heart, he teaches people from a background of an outdoorsman, public administrator, Hall of Fame fisherman, college professor, businessman, community leader, and pastor. He has served in the capacity of a chaplain with the San Francisco 49ers, the Oakland Raiders, Hurricane Katrina, and the Post Falls Idaho Police Department. His life experiences, study of discipleship, and work with hundreds of churches have given him a unique perspective on helping men to know God and make Him known.

His passion is to serve our Lord and assist others to know Him in a great way. Grassi is available as a keynote speaker, church ministry consultant, men's ministry leader, and life coach to those seeking assistance in developing a vision and life plan. Through his ministry website, www.mensministrycatalyst.org, he can be contacted for speaking engagements and assistance in developing your life plan.

RESOURCES AVAILABLE

Men's Ministry Catalyst: Resources available through MMC, www.mensministrycatalyst.org.

Weekly Devotionals for Men: Ideal for pastors and men's leaders to e-mail to their men.

http://www.mensministrycatalyst.org/stay-informed/devotional-archives/

MMC Library of Best Practices: Especially designed to assist leaders, available at (208) 457-9619.

MMC Hotline (208) 457-9619: Call anytime for assistance on creating ministry to men.

Monthly Men's Ministry Newsletter: This monthly e-mail newsletter gives you tips and techniques on how to equip, inspire, and motivate men for kingdom purposes, available at www.mensministrycatalyst.org.

Dr. James Grassi as a speaker, coach, and equipper for individuals, men's leaders, and churches http://www.romans12disciple.org

SOCIAL MEDIA

http://www.mensministrycatalyst.org/our-blog

http://www.romans12disciple.org

http://www.facebook.com/MensMinistryCatalyst

http://twitter.com/MensMinCatalyst

http://www.youtube.com/user/MensMinCatalyst

Personal Church Consulting: We will send a church consultant to your location; call (208) 457-9619

Men's Ministry Catalyst Website: www.mensministrycatalyst.org

KNOW YOURSELF, HONOR OTHERS, LIVE FOR CHRIST

CHECK OUT THE OTHER BOOKS IN THE SERIES

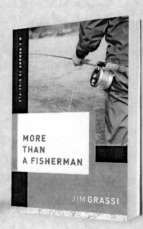

Discover what it means to live for Christ. Learn how to fully surrender yourself over to God. Rescue not only your faith, but also others.

THOMAS NELSON
Since 1798

CPSIA information can be obtained
at www.ICGtesting.com
Printed in the USA
LVOW07s0535081217
558733LV00018B/171/P